Schools Without Fear

A realistic guide to tackling bullying as a whole school issue

**By Nick Boddington
and Noreen Wetton**

fp FORBES PUBLICATIONS

Schools without fear
By Noreen Wetton and
Nick Boddington

© Forbes Publications 1998

Design by X-Design

Published by Forbes Publications
Abbott House
1-2 Hanover Street
London W1R 9WB

Tel: 0171 495 7945
Fax: 0171 495 7916

Printed in Great Britain by
St Edmundsbury Press Ltd,
Bury St Edmunds, Suffolk

Acknowledgments

We would like to thank all of the schools and teachers whose comments and ideas have contributed to this book.

We would especially like to thank the staff and children of:

Whitmore Junior School – Basildon
Chelmer Valley GM Secondary School – Chelmsford
Spinney Junior School – Harlow
Tiptree Heath School – Tiptree
Deneholm Primary School – Thurrock
Westcliff County High School for Girls

We would also like to thank all the authors, teachers and colleagues who have over the years shaped our thinking and offered us their 'good ideas'. If we have forgotten to acknowledge anyone, our sincerest apologies!

Contents

INTRODUCTION   **PAGE 4**

CHAPTER ONE
AN EFFECTIVE FOCUS   **PAGE 7**

CHAPTER TWO
DEFINE 'BULLYING'   **PAGE 16**

CHAPTER THREE
EXPLORING THE WHOLE SCHOOL ETHOS   **PAGE 37**

CHAPTER FOUR
ADDRESS INCIDENTS OF BULLYING   **PAGE 57**

CHAPTER FIVE
BUILD A CURRICULUM   **PAGE 92**

CONCLUSION   **PAGE 105**

BIBLIOGRAPHY   **PAGE 106**

INTRODUCTION

Welcome...

SO WHY HAVE YOU PICKED UP THIS BOOK?

How have you arrived at this page? Did you, like most people, skim backwards through the book before arriving at this page, or are you the type of person who starts at the front and works forward? Either way the chances are, you are reading this book for one or more of the following reasons:

- A parent is telling you that her or his child is being bullied
- A child tells you he, she or a friend is being bullied
- You are confronted by an incident of bullying in your school, or possibly involving your own child, and you need to consider how to stop it – and keep it stopped
- You believe that bullying is taking place in your school
- You have an anxiety that all relationships in the school are not quite as healthy as you would like
- You have been asked to formulate a policy to address incidents of bullying and you are looking for a sense of direction
- You think that your school is free from bullying and you want to ensure that it stays that way... and of course you may be wrong
- You just feel strongly about the issue and want to ensure that children in your school do not suffer the pain of being bullied

The chances are that you will also recall incidents of being bullied or even, in hindsight, admit to having bullied others. It would not surprise us if deep down you share with us very strong feelings about bullying and a desire to ensure that, as far as possible, our schools are warm and safe environments where children feel secure and are able to learn effectively. If we are to achieve or maintain this positive school culture we need to tackle not only actual bullying, but the fear of bullying. Ideally we want a school culture where the idea of bullying or being bullied simply doesn't occur to the children.

We also need to take account of the children who, for many and varied reasons believe, or say, they are being bullied in school. A report from a child or parent of a young person 'being bullied' could cover many fears, concerns or activities and yet not fall within our immediate definitions of being bullied.

WHAT IS THIS BOOK ABOUT?

This book is intended to offer a model for planning how to make your school one which does not tolerate bullying by:

- **Staff – of each other and other children**
- **Children/pupils/students**
- **People who work in and around the school, formally, informally, regularly, invited, uninvited and that helps children who are the target of, or believe they are the target of bullying**

THIS BOOK FITS INTO FOUR BROAD SECTIONS:

1) **Setting the scene** – to consider exactly what it is we are trying to address and how we can find out about what is going on in our school.

2) **The whole school ethos** – to consider how the climate of the school can be altered to minimise bullying behaviour. This will include practical ways to 'engineer out' opportunities for bullying behaviour to take place.

3) **Incident management** – to consider how we will manage immediate incidents of bullying behaviour or what is described as bullying behaviour.

4) **The curriculum** or addressing bullying as part of the classroom programme, to consider the contribution that the taught curriculum can offer both to exploring incidents of bullying behaviour and ways of coping with such aggression.

When someone asks 'What do you do about bullying?',

you can say 'here it is, in our curriculum', before

bullying happens

The strand of recognising and preventing bullying should be a properly planned and clearly visible part of the personal, social, moral and health education curriculum from four years of age upwards. It needs to be visible to all and, perhaps, to children most of all. When someone asks 'What do you do about bullying?', whether you are a nursery or a tertiary college you can say 'here it is, in our curriculum' before bullying happens. In this respect it should be no different from the school's approach to drug or sex education.

WHO IS THIS BOOK WRITTEN FOR?

This book is written for teachers, teaching assistants, school managers and governors, mid-day assistants and parents. Don't look just in the sections that seem to apply mostly to your phase of education. Lots of what you will find is about children, whether you call them that, or young people or pupils or students (throughout this book we will use 'children').

It is about people, places, feelings and language and it could all apply, with just a little modification, to your class or school. This is why we haven't put labels on things. We don't know your class, school, environment or community and the talents, skills and problems you and they have.

You do and will take from the book what you think will work best for you, develop and extend it. When, if ever, we see or hear what you have done with it we will probably kick ourselves for not having come up with your ideas.

CHAPTER ONE

An effective focus

While we will spend time in this book considering some strategies or models for addressing incidents in both primary and secondary schools, these come in later chapters. You could think of these as short term strategies. If all you do, however, is design a procedure or protocol for managing incidents of bullying, then be sure to keep them handy, because it is likely that you will be using them quite frequently!

It is our intention to make this book as practical and realistic as possible. Because this book is largely for teachers and school managers we have to acknowledge that the amount of time that any member of staff can give to addressing an incident of bullying is very limited. Because of this we need to ensure that this time is used as effectively as possible.

Many teachers we have worked with tell us that addressing an obvious incident of bullying is easier than the 'third party' or 'hearsay' reports of bullying. We will look at ways of exploring this later.

This book is very clear about the role, responsibilities and boundaries that lie around the work of teachers. It is not intended to enable teachers to become educational psychologists, educational welfare officers, social workers or even police officers, although at times we are required to take on some aspects of all of these roles! Bullying is not an issue that any one teacher can address alone; it is an issue for the whole school community. There may come a time when an incident of bullying goes beyond the resources and expertise of the school community and we need to draw in support from the wider community. This moment is likely to be unique to each individual school. This is not unique to bullying and staff should never see the need to refer beyond the school as a failure.

This book is intended to help schools fulfil their own role as effectively as possible, within the resources that are available to them, while acknowledging that there will be times when we will need to refer to or work alongside colleagues from other professions. If we do not acknowledge these boundaries we are in danger of drowning in the enormity of what is possible, becoming immobilised, or trying to adopt a role we really know little about and making matters worse. The children in our care will benefit very little if any of this happens.

But it is not enough to simply have a procedure for addressing incidents, nor telling children that if they are bullied, the school will listen and support them. There are other, more important considerations:

- **We need to consider how we create a whole school climate or ethos which minimises the climate where 'bullying' takes place.**
- **We need to ensure that if children experience being bullied, they both know that they can ask for help and are enabled to ask for help.**
- **We need to ensure that children have the language with which to express themselves and are confident and becoming practised in using that language.**

When we approach the issue of bullying, we also need to check out our language. Telling young children in an assembly that the school does not tolerate 'bullying' may not make a link in the child's mind with the behaviour that they are experiencing. We need to explore the area in some detail with children in order to ensure that all members of our school community agree and understand what behaviours are unacceptable whether or not we call

> My headteacher talks about 'bullying' during assembly, my parents talk about 'teasing', the others in my class say calling me names is only 'joking'. I just feel rotten and confused, but is this what the headteacher is talking about... am I being bullied...?

them bullying. Telling young people that bullying will not be tolerated in the school is no help for the child who is being bullied or is afraid that he or she will be.

Treating the child who has summoned up the courage to go and tell someone he or she is being bullied as a 'teller of tales' is worse than no help. It makes the victim, or the child who thinks he or she is a victim, into the transgressor.

As Celeste reminds her teacher in Anne Fine's book, *The Angel of Nitshill Road*, the rule not to tell tales was invented by bullies and the people who don't really want to stand up to them.

There needs to be a huge change in the perceptions of every person who works in the school and that 'telling tales' is not the way to describe what children tell. This culture of 'telling tales' dies hard and perhaps even more so than we expect and perhaps mostly with people who work in the school in a non-teaching role. Perhaps we need a note in our school policy that the term 'telling tales' is not used in this school!

It is not enough to say to children that they should tell someone immediately. We need to enable children to tell others and to ask for help. The teacher needs to understand the children's language. We need to know what words children use that encompass bullying. We also need to be aware of 'volume', that the whispered words 'she is bothering me' from a child can sound 'soft' to a teacher, but in the absence of an appropriate language and high self-esteem, the child

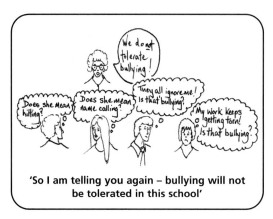

'So I am telling you again – bullying will not be tolerated in this school'

is actually screaming 'she is bullying me!'

We need to spend time helping children explore the difference between 'having a moan', 'having a complain' and 'reporting that they are being hurt'. We can't just assume that this happens naturally.

It is not enough just to say we are a listening school; we need to be pro-active in checking out if everything is okay. If we do not do this, we are relying on children to have the confidence to ask staff for help, with all of the potential consequences, many of which may be uncertain or frightening that this may hold. This seems a little inappropriate when children who are being bullied may, by definition, be feeling anxious, powerless, vulnerable and perhaps even worthless. If we are on the sharp end of systematic abuse then we are hardly likely to be at our 'problem solving best'!

It is not surprising that many children have reached a stage of desperation before they seek help. It is sad that some children who receive bullying resort, perhaps through panic, to inappropriate behaviours themselves, whether self harm or exploding into a burst of temper in order to attract attention and support.

This book includes both 'crisis management strategies' and an exploration of some medium and longer term strategies towards creating a climate where bullying behaviour is reduced.

Bullying behaviour never goes completely away, which is why addressing it needs to be planned into the curriculum. Bullying behaviour is not something that the school can say it has addressed and can leave behind and now move on. Each year a new group of children will join the school, each bringing a particular background and experiences. New staff will join the school and they will need to learn the school's culture and ethos and understand the school's approach to bullying behaviour.

In our research for this book, we were struck by the strength the perceived school culture has on children's perceptions of how their school addresses bullying. We have heard children say:

There is no point in telling the teachers, they can't do anything and things only get worse. It's no good telling the dinner ladies. They don't do anything. They say to ignore it, it's just a bit of fun

Even more depressing is that similar views have been presented by groups of parents:

Even the teachers are frightened of the big students. I have told my son to hit back hard and I will support him all the way

In both cases, the schools in question were very caring and had good track records of quietly supporting children and addressing the very few actual incidents of bullying. This perception of the school's culture is often built on a 'mythology' of historical incidents, some of which are fictitious, of how the school has or has not dealt with previous incidents of bullying.

Failing to tackle this 'mythology' can prevent a school moving forward with this issue. Sadly, it is human nature for the school's successes to carry far less weight than the school's failures. If we are going to break a perception of a school that can't help, we must try to ensure as rigorous and consistent an approach to addressing bullying as possible.

During the writing of this book, we have become even more convinced that addressing bullying should be a high profile collaboration with the whole school community and that the process should be as open and as honest as possible.

As we work together through this book, we will pose questions for you to consider. In many cases there will not be a 'right answer', although we will offer our views. We hope that by working through these points, your own position and perhaps the framework for a whole school policy will emerge.

A good starting point is to consider bullying as an equal opportunities issue. Put simply, frightened children are unlikely to learn as effectively as happy and safe children. If you are:

- Afraid to attend school
- Terrified of the playground
- Scared of going into the toilets
- Frightened of the journey home
- Anxious about working in groups
- Constantly being told you are not as good as others
- Picked on
- Teased and laughed at

you are not getting your share of the taught curriculum. If this is further compounded by being treated unsympathetically by teachers because the standard of your work is now suffering, we have a fairly clear equality of opportunities issue!

If children are receiving long term, systematic bullying in, at worse, an apparently uncaring or indifferent environment, expecting them to do their best work and achieve their highest results at the same time is asking quite a lot.

But as professionals we also have responsibilities towards children who bully others. The Education Reform Act charges us with providing a curriculum which:

'Prepares children for the responsibilities,
opportunities and experiences of adult life.'

So we must do everything in our power to attempt to modify this behaviour. We need to ensure that we give equal attention to all parties involved in incidents of bullying. The consequences of unchecked bullying behaviour can be appalling for the bully, the 'hangers on' who collude, the bullied and the witnesses.

There is research evidence to suggest that as many as 25% of aggressive children grow up into aggressive adults (*Olweus 1984*) and that a number of adult problems are significantly associated with aggressive behaviour in childhood. For many young chronic bullies, both male and female, the outlook can be quite bleak.

There is no doubt that the investment in time required to create a whole school ethos that discourages bullying behaviour is considerable. However, this ethos will inevitably have a positive impact on many other aspects of the life of the school.

Finally, there is a wider issue. If we believe that bullying behaviour is unacceptable, should we not be trying to provide children with an education that enables them to live and work together in constructive relationships where bullying behaviour is seen by all to be inappropriate and inefficient?

Above and opposite: Examples of 'bubble dialogues' or cartoons of situations, with the speech bubbles either left blank, or with one character asking a prompting question, so that the child can respond through a second character

CHAPTER TWO

Define bullying

Our first step is to check out that we are all talking about the same thing. Many of the words we use, especially in personal, social and health education, have a habit of 'rolling off the tongue' but are actually very hard to define with any accuracy. (For example, try defining the words 'health' and 'healthy'!)

It is surprising but true that the word 'bullying' is very hard to define. We considered trying to find another word for it, because of the stereotyping it may create. We seriously considered trying to find another set of words, such as:

It is almost impossible and whatever we call it, children and parents will use the words bullying and bully to describe those kinds of behaviours which make them feel intimidated, harmed, humiliated or uncomfortable.

Any child can, at some stage of life, be the victim of other's aggressive behaviour and any child can, at times, behave in aggressive ways towards others. Labelling children, whilst tempting, is not helpful. A child who is simply and perhaps publicly labelled a bully may see that as a position of power and try to live up to it, especially if self-esteem is so low that success in this behaviour is personally rewarding. Equally, labelling children as a 'victim' can

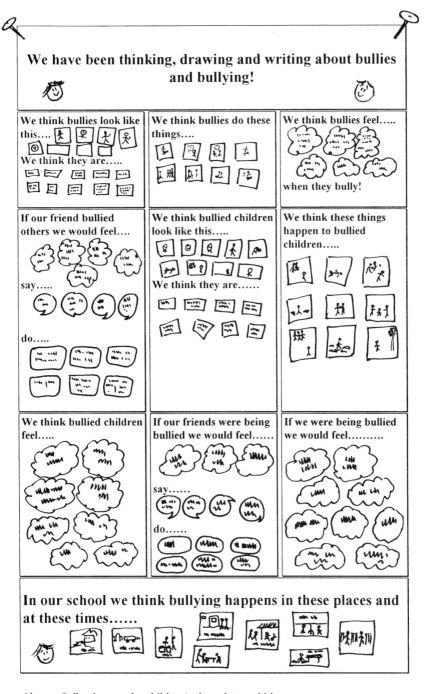

We have been thinking, drawing and writing about bullies and bullying!

We think bullies look like this....
We think they are.....

We think bullies do these things....

We think bullies feel.....
when they bully!

If our friend bullied others we would feel....
say.....
do.....

We think bullied children look like this.....
We think they are......

We think these things happen to bullied children.....

We think bullied children feel.....

If our friends were being bullied we would feel......
say......
do......

If we were being bullied we would feel..........

In our school we think bullying happens in these places and at these times......

Above: Collecting up the children's thoughts and ideas

serve to further disempower them, especially at a time when they are likely to already be feeling fairly powerless.

Whilst we could quote many dictionary definitions of bullying, perhaps the only really important definition is the one that makes sense to you, your colleagues, your pupils and others in your community.

What does the word 'bullying' mean to you? Try defining it in one sentence. The chances are that you found this quite hard. The more you think about this term, the more complex it becomes. Did you think of bullying as:

- **An older or bigger person physically harming another smaller or younger person, or could it be the other way round?**
- **Verbal as well as physical attack?**
- **Systematic repeated incidents or any 'one-off' incident?**
- **A group on to one individual or an individual on to an individual?**
- **Damage to a person, or damage to that person's work or property?**
- **Dramatic incidents or events, or small scale, insidious incidents?**
- **A malicious, knowing intent to cause harm or misery, or acts of teasing or thoughtlessness?**
- **Cutting out or ignoring someone?**
- **Making someone feel unwanted, especially when they have once been friends?**
- **Persistent putting down through the use of sarcasm?**
- **Teaching through creating a fear in children of 'getting it wrong'?**

You might like to try doing this activity with your colleagues, possibly as part of a staff workshop.

One way to think about bullying is to consider that it may look different and be defined differently depending on your viewpoint. Consider a young person who is being systematically jostled by a group of peers in the playground, corridors and on the stairs. The group is led by one individual who initiates the bullying behaviour. Finally, the recipient lashes out at the main source of the assaults.

- **The bully may see his or her actions as simply fun and think it amusing to jostle another person and seek to justify it by saying the recipient 'needs to learn how to take a joke'**
- **The co-bullies in the group may see their actions as keeping them within the group, or helping to avoid becoming targets themselves**
- **The recipient may experience feelings of constant dread**
- **The teacher or witness may just see an accidental nudge with a shoulder being responded to in a completely inappropriate manner**

Unfortunately, many acts of bullying that teachers witness are only one event in a long line of incidents. Without investigation, the victim of systematic long term bullying who finally snaps may suddenly be disciplined by a member of staff, sometimes in front of the bullies, which is not very constructive.

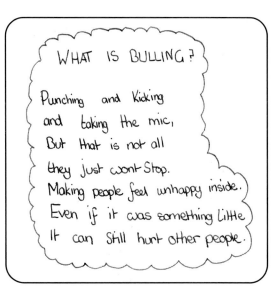

WHAT IS BULLING?

Punching and Kicking
and taking the mic,
But that is not all
they just wont stop.
Making people feel unhappy inside.
Even if it was something little
It can still hurt other people.

FINDING OUT WHAT OUR YOUNG PEOPLE THINK BULLYING IS AND HOW THEY SHOW IT IN WORDS AND PICTURES

A good starting point for creating a policy is to explore with everyone in the school community what is meant by the term 'bully', 'being bullied' and 'bullies'. You could try using some illuminative research activities. These can be a good way into exploring a whole variety of sensitive issues.

With children of all ages, carrying out draw and write investigations may be one approach to exploring the starting points for bullying. Other activities might include using 'bubble sheets' (sheets covered in outlines of 'thought bubbles' or 'speech bubbles' to explore children's starting points). Another approach is to prepare 'bubble dialogues' or cartoons of situations, with the speech bubbles either left blank, or with one character asking a prompting question, so that the child can respond through a second character.

All these strategies are illuminative but lend themselves to being quantified. Indeed, the pupils can take part in the quantification. Illuminative research strategies give powerful insights into pupils, changing perceptions of bullies, bullying and being bullied. They also give insights into the language which pupils themselves may use. This is clearly important for helping you to understand the child who is seeking your help but has poor language skills.

Children who are young, have not yet mastered writing for themselves, or children with varied and special needs can take part in illuminative research strategies with the help of teachers or classroom assistants who can act as scribe, writing down what the child whispers to them but not adding to it in any way.

With older children in secondary schools, using tutorial or PSE time to explore what the school community considers to be bullying, can be a useful starting point.

At the end of this chapter, we offer schools a way into exploring children's perceptions of bullying. The questionnaire sheets on pages 32 to 36 can be enlarged on a photocopier and given to the children. We have also included detailed instructions to follow closely. It is important that these are followed; the wording has been carefully chosen to begin by distancing the investigation from the individual children by using fictitious people. The names are as neutral as we can make them so that they do not, for example, appear to imply, identify or exclude ethnic groups. Only gradually during the research process are pupils asked directly what they would feel, say and do. The pace of the investigation needs to be slow enough to encourage real reflection.

If the children can't draw, the teacher will have to draw at their specific instruction, being prepared to alter or abandon her drawings if these do not fit the children's views. The teacher will have to resist making any suggestions other than 'like this?'.

> *The names are as neutral as we can make them so that they do not, for example, appear to imply, identify or exclude ethnic groups*

When we first used this research tool, some children found it hard to 'describe' a bully or bullied person. The idea of 'describing something' hints at the need for a page of writing, which may inhibit many children. One variation that was suggested to us was to just ask children to list the words they would associate with each question. (Don't forget to be tolerant of strong language!)

When the research has been completed, the children are likely to want and need a chance to talk about their work.

If you are using the strategy as research, it is essential to ensure that, as far as possible, children have opportunities to work alone. It is important to gather individual children's thoughts, rather than, through discussion, creating a composite picture of the class's worst thoughts and fears. There is a danger that without children working alone, the issue gets 'talked up' into an inaccurate picture. This is one time when 'test conditions' can be really helpful. Teachers can reassure children by explaining:

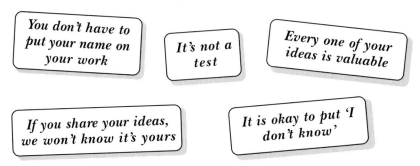

You don't have to put your name on your work

It's not a test

Every one of your ideas is valuable

If you share your ideas, we won't know it's yours

It is okay to put 'I don't know'

This can be used as a research strategy or spread over a number of class activities.

LOOKING AT THE RESULTS

You can learn a lot with your first look through the response sheets. Try to get a general sense of what they are telling you. Is it positive or negative? Do any stereotypes 'shout out' at you?

Now look again. It is too easy to be pulled in different directions by the wealth of information. Focus on the writing by the drawings, box by box, clarifying what categories of response you are looking for. We offer a suggested analysis framework, but you will probably want to add your own categories.

What did the children tell you?

- How do they perceive a 'bully'? What are the characteristics that appear dominant? Are they large, violent, ordinary, spiteful, ugly?
- What are bullied children perceived to be like? Are they small, different, from a minority group?
- What do the children think bullies do?

- **What do the children think has happened to the bullied?**
- **What are the bullies and bullied feeling throughout this?**
- **How do the children feel?**

When you got closer to the children themselves, what were their feelings? Did they have constructive strategies, in terms of things to say and positive helpful things to do? On reflection, did they appear to have either nothing to say, unhelpful comments or a set of ideas for action that would make the problem ten times worse?

The following pages look at just a little of the information that Whitmore Junior School in Basildon gathered from carrying out this type of activity with children aged 9-10 years.

How we describe a 'bully'

They offered us a range of images and language that they associated with bullies. We expected some stereotyping, for example, drawings of big strong people, or aggressive clothing or hair cuts, but in most of the drawings the bullies were drawn virtually the same as the bullied children. The most common language was nasty, horrible, selfish. Many children said that bullies think they are strong, but none said they felt bullies actually were strong. The number of children who drew male bullies and victims of bullying were virtually the same as the number who drew female bullies and victims. These children also linked the sex of the bully with the same sex victim.

'We think bullies do...'

These children thought bullies physically hurt you, were rude to you, or threatened you. A number of children used language that suggested intrusion into your life. They said 'it could carry on for days... they follow you...' Others identified feeling trapped, 'they hold you against the wall ...they push you to the ground and sit on you.' Surprisingly this group of children did not identify any one set of bullying behaviours with a particular gender.

'When bullies are doing this, we think they feel...'
This group of children thought bullies felt a range of emotions, but they seemed to fall into two groups: positive feelings 'big, tough, proud' and negative feelings, 'very, very, very cross and angry, sad,

grumpy'. These children appeared to recognise that bullying is motivated by a variety of feelings in other people and many appeared quite sympathetic to the bully, whilst wanting them to stop. Others identified a coldness in the bully, a feeling of 'fine and refreshed, like nothing has happened'. A number identified peer acceptance and approval, saying the bully felt 'best, because they have all their mates'. Once again, positive and negative feelings were spread across both genders.

Whitmore School gathered a wealth of information from this activity. Perhaps most disturbing was the children's perception of the type of person who is most likely to be the victim of bullying. They described the victim as being:

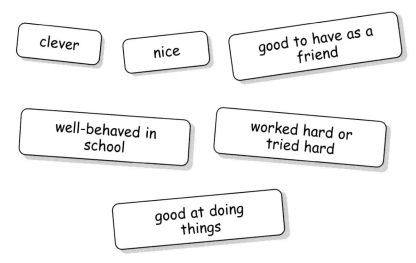

Sadly, it seemed that the type of young person the school was aspiring to develop was being identified by the young people as the sort of person who was most vulnerable to being bullied!

What we can do with what we learn?
There is a powerful opportunity here to do a number of things. Perhaps the first step might be to take all the children's feelings back to the group and help them to share them. It is important for

children to understand that their feelings are not isolated and that many of their peers feel the same way about the issue of bullying. There is an opportunity here to help children to enhance their vocabulary with regard to feelings. This may help in a later confrontation with a bully, and certainly in an appeal for help to an adult.

It might then be useful to discuss with the children the images that they offered for bullies and the types of behaviour that they associate with bullying.

If the children have a very narrow view of what constitutes bullying, for example, physical violence only, go back to their work on the feelings of bullied people. Ask the children to think about other ways in which someone could make another person have that kind of feeling. If these behaviours or actions also make people feel like this, might these also be bullying? In this way, it is possible to encourage the children to expand their concept of appropriate and inappropriate behaviour.

When the children were asked to draw and write about what the bullies did and what happened to the bullied young person, did you get any insights into times – for example, break, lunch, on the way to and from school – or locations such as the playground, toilets, corridors? If so, what action could you take to address this?

Because this question was not part of our original investigation, these 'risky places' were explored in follow-up discussions, but it would be easy to include a question in the draw and write activity that asked individuals to record where they think the two 'bullies' might carry out bullying and where the two bullied children may have been bullied.

How do the children feel about being the friend of a bully or a person who is being bullied? Again, what are their strategies? Can they think of something that might stop the bullying, or do they feel they might join in? There are a number of opportunities to consider how they might act if they witness an incident of bullying.

Do the children think doing nothing is going to help? Why do

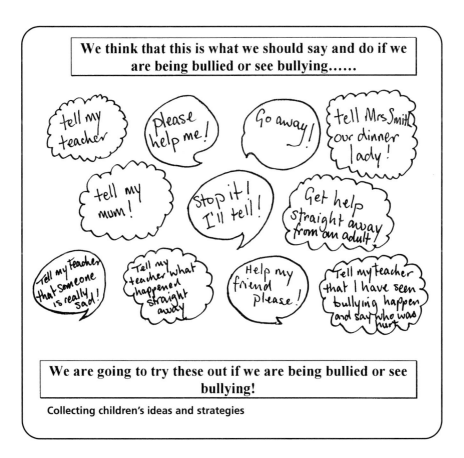

Collecting children's ideas and strategies

some children not want to get involved? We need to acknowledge that getting help is sometimes difficult. It might be more constructive to say, ' Telling someone is difficult. How would you make an adult stop and listen?' Once we have some ideas, it might be a good time to practice some of them.

Depressingly, many adults witnessing an assault in the wider community don't want to get involved, even in summoning help, so it is asking a lot to demand this of children without investigating the issues, exploring and offering some possible strategies.

If they were being bullied, did the children say that they would tell someone? Who did they identify? It is usually a parent or a teacher, but sometimes different people are identified. If it is a mid-day assistant are the children saying they would wait until lunch time, or are they indicating the playground is a place where bullying takes place?

In our pilot study most younger children said they would only 'tell their mum' if they felt they were being bullied. This may account for why many incidents of bullying are reported first from the home. Working with parents is really important and we have found using children's drawings and writings as the starting point for parents' sessions on bullying to be very useful. Many schools hold sessions to look at a range of sensitive issues and a session on bullying fits naturally into this process.

We know it can be hard getting parents to attend these sessions, they can be stormy, a lot of anecdotes usually get told and a lot of

> *Working with parents is really important and we have found using children's drawings and writings as the starting point for parents' sessions on bullying to be very useful*

'baggage gets dumped' but once we have worked through these, the positive discussions they generate and that can follow in the community can be helpful. It does send a message that the school is taking the issue seriously and, if it goes well, can help to encourage more parents to attend future pastoral sessions.

Parents need to recognise that when a young person says that they are being bullied, this may cover a wide range of behaviours all of which need to be taken seriously and addressed swiftly. Whilst not wishing to swamp a school with approaches from parents, it is usually easier for the school to deal with a problem if it is reported quickly and doesn't have the time to escalate. Parents' sessions can help explore this balance and agree as to what warning signs need to be reported to the school.

Make sure that you keep in mind that you have asked children to use their imaginations to project into someone else's point of view. For some children, we may be tapping into actual events and experiences. For many, we may be tapping into fears about imagined future events. Addressing both is valuable, since as we have indicated, fear gets in the way of learning, and exploring appropriate strategies before an event is usually a better plan than picking up the pieces afterwards.

There is an opportunity here to try another activity. With the children's permission, their responses can be shared with and discussed with older children. Their drawings and written statements can be a very powerful and direct way to open discussion on or confront the topic of bullying. It can also be an interesting activity for a primary school to share year 6 responses with both the staff and students of a feeder secondary school.

Without investigations using this type of exercise, it is likely that your anti-bullying policy will mean different things to different people. If one of the most important aspects of a bullying policy is that everyone knows:

- **Their rights**
- **Their responsibilities**
- **Which actions are appropriate**
- **Which actions are inappropriate**
- **What the consequences of inappropriate action will be**

then it is important that everyone agrees what bullying means in your particular school.

Schools without fear

A draw and write investigation into young people's perceptions of bullies and the victims of bullying

INSTRUCTIONS FOR TEACHERS

Either photocopy and enlarge the sheets on **pages 32-36** or hand copy them exactly as shown. Each child will eventually need one set each, although you may wish to spread the activity over a number of sessions.

Because you want to gain an insight into each individual child's understanding and feelings, tell the children that this work is different from their normal work.

Now say:

'Good morning, class. Today we are going to find out what you think about children who bully other children and children who are bullied.

'I am going to ask you to do some drawing and some writing. I am not going to ask you to put your names on these sheets, but I would like you to write on the back if you are a boy or a girl and your age. Turn your sheet over and do this now.'

When the children have done this, say:

'Now turn the sheet back over.

'There are no right or wrong drawings or answers. Everyone's work and ideas are equally important and equally valuable. It

is also all right to say "I don't know" if you can't think of anything to write.

'Because I want to know what you think, I don't want you to share your ideas or work with anyone else.

'If you want to write something down and you don't know how to spell it, put your hand up and I will come and help you.

'Look at the top left corner of page one. You will see there is a number one with a ring around it.'

Read the instructions and ask them to draw Sam or Jo. When the first children appear to finish say:

'When you have finished your drawing you can colour it in **(this allows other children to finish their pencil drawings)** *but if you don't finish colouring, don't worry; you will have some time at the end.'*

When all the children have finished their drawings say:

'Good, well done. Now look at the box next to your drawing.'

Read out the instructions in box 2.

If any children need help, write down for them what they want to say. Write exactly what they tell you, nothing more or less. Continue with the rest of the exercise in the same fashion.

1

1) Sam and Jo are both bullies. Choose one of them and draw what you think they look like.

2) If you were telling someone about what kind of people they are, what would you say they are like?

3) Choose either Sam or Jo and draw what you think they might have done.

4) If you were telling someone about them, what sort of things would you say they did?

5) Draw a picture to show how you think Sam or Jo felt when they were bullying.

6) Write down how you think Sam or Jo felt when they were bullying.

1) If you were Sam or Jo's friend, what would you feel?

I would feel...

2) What would you say?

I would say...

3) What would you do?

I would....

3

1) Mel and Terry are being bullied. Choose one of them and draw what you think they look like.

2) If you were telling someone about what kind of people they are, what would you say?

3) Choose Mel or Terry and draw what you think might have happened to them.

4) If you were telling someone about them, what sort of things would you say had happened to them?

5) Draw a picture to show how Mel or Terry felt when they were being bullied.

6) Write down how you think Mel or Terry felt when they were being bullied.

1) If you were Mel or Terry's friend, what would you feel like?

I would feel....

2) What would you say?

I would say...

3) What would you do?

I would....

5

1) If you were being bullied, how would you feel?

I would feel...

2) What would you say?

I would say....

3) What would you do?

I would...

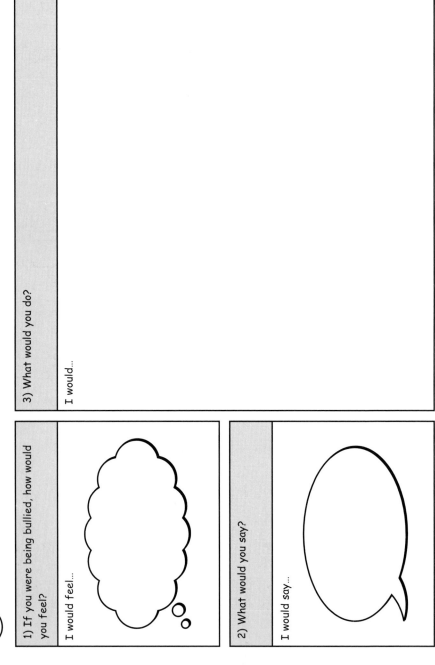

CHAPTER THREE

Exploring the whole school ethos

There is no doubt that children are concerned about bullying or the fear of being bullied.

We asked 96 children in year 7 two simple, open ended questions:

1) What makes you comfortable to learn?

2) What makes you uncomfortable, not so comfortable, to learn?

For 48% of children, bullying was highlighted as a factor that made learning more difficult.

If we want to create a school that doesn't tolerate bullying, it might be easier to turn the problem upside down and consider what a school environment would look like that made bullying really easy. (This activity is adapted from an exercise offered by Michele Elliot.)

Begin by asking everyone in the school community to contribute to creating a picture or description of a pretend school where bullying can easily take place and where bullies can really enjoy themselves.

You might like to try offering some prompts:

- *What type of places would we find?*
- *What would teachers say and do?*
- *What would pupils say and do?*
- *What would happen at break and lunch time?*
- *What would happen in the corridors?*
- *What would happen in classrooms?*
- *What would parents or carers say and do?*
- *How would different groups of people feel?*

This could be done through:

- **Staff meetings (don't forget to invite all the staff)**
- **Year meetings**
- **Governor meetings**
- **Tutorial periods in secondary schools**
- **A general class discussion in a PSE, English or RE lesson**
- **Drawings and follow up discussion**
- **School council meetings**
- **An invitation to parents**
- **Assemblies**

Once this 'rich picture' has been created, we need to offer it to the school community and ask questions. First of all:

What parts of this picture can be found in our school at the moment?

This can be fascinating, but perhaps most interesting are the matches and mis-matches between different groups within and outside the school community. For example, there can be a considerable difference between the aspects identified by the staff and the younger children!

The next question is obvious:

What could we all do to put this right?

This can offer a clear set of action points in which everyone feels they have some ownership.

What has come up before?

From previous experience with schools that have worked through this type of process, a number of headings or clusters of issues have emerged:

- **The way people talk to each other and about each other, including the inappropriate use of nicknames or labels**
- **Supportive relationships between all members of the school community**
- **The safe and not so safe places**
- **The safe and not so safe times in the passage of the day**
- **The way people approach and report incidents**
- **The need for more co-operative work to be planned into class activity and an emphasis being placed on social skills**

A number of schools have taken up the notion of trying to 'engineer out' opportunities for bullying to take place. It would be naive to suggest that this solves the problem, but it can go a significant way to reducing it.

For example, one infant school noticed that children were always pushing to the front in the dinner queue. Rather than solve this by discipline, the mid-day assistant arranged for the children to form a circle on the playground with her in the middle. Each day a different child leads in!

Codes of conduct and language

The way teachers, support staff and peers talk to children and the language they use can have a profound effect on their self esteem. It is very easy to let comments that are overheard by teachers go unchallenged. This can give the impression that the teacher is colluding with those children who may be, even only mildly, taunting another pupil. Not only does this damage the trust of the person being taunted but may also give tacit permission to the 'taunters' to continue. If the comments are unchallenged, it then raises the question: when does it reach a level of unacceptability that requires a teacher to intervene?

As a starting point, we need to examine how we generally talk to and listen to everyone in the school. Do we demonstrate that each person is an equally valuable member of the school and try to spend time listening to each other's news?

Do we, through the curriculum, encourage children to develop a language that enables them to communicate their feelings to us, and to express their feelings to others in assertive ways? We need to ensure that there are aspects of the curriculum which specifically set out to extend the children's language of feelings.

We need to find ways to ensure that children understand that we will listen to them, and that this is a normal part of relations within the school, not just something that happens when you are in trouble and in need of help. It is far less likely that inappropriate name calling or hurtful language will take place in an environment where children are encouraged, through role modelling, to use language that values or affirms others' worth.

A number of secondary and primary schools have developed various techniques to address language in the school. Many encourage staff to use tutorial or class time to construct 'classroom rules', and some have gone further to construct a

Establishing playground rules can be a valuable lesson in compromise for the whole school

whole school set of agreed appropriate behaviour.

A simple activity used by one primary school was to involve supervisory staff getting each class to individually agree on their three most important rules for the playground. These were then exchanged between classes and discussed. The rules for year 6 turned out to be the reverse of those agreed by the reception class. Year 6 said 'Little ones should keep out of the way so we can play'. Reception said 'Big ones should let us have our bit of the playground'. This was quite a shock to year 6 and a lot of negotiation had to take place in order to arrive at three rules that everyone felt were fair!

'Our three rules for our playground' were displayed in each classroom and at all the exits from the building to the playground. Any 'rule breakers' were then asked to identify which rule they had broken.

If well managed, 'circle time' offers an ideal opportunity to explore feelings about language and set agreements about acceptable language and behaviour. (See *Feeling Good – Raising Children's Self Esteem in the Classroom* – Wetton and Cansell, and *Turning*

Our names are really important to us. Many

people find it really irritating to be referred to by

the wrong name, a shortened version of our name

or a 'nickname' we have not chosen

Your School Round – Mosley, as good starting points for this type of activity.)

The advantage of an agreed whole school policy, produced in a format that is accessible to everyone, is that a teacher can immediately say: 'Wait a minute, we all agreed that talking like this to one another is not acceptable. If it continues there will be consequences and these will be...' The teacher might also want to spend some time separately with both the taunters and the recipient, taking apart exactly what is going on.

A word of caution: school codes of behaviour must be constantly used. They must be 'living documents', part of the day-to-day interaction in the school. If they are not, they quickly become valueless. It is also important to remember that the children who were involved in the process of formulating the policy will see them quite differently from new children who, even after discussion, may just have to abide by them. Codes of behaviour need to be reviewed and reworked, especially if children tell you a rule isn't working.

The process of formulating an agreed way of working is important, so classes need to continue to explore their own ways of working, even if they are within previously established school code.

Names

Love them or hate them, our names are really important to us. Many people find it really irritating to be referred to by the wrong name, a shortened version of our name or a 'nickname' we have not chosen. We need to be very careful about the way we refer to children. It is one matter to call a young person by a preferred name, but quite another to adopt a nickname selected by peers. It is always worth checking out with a young person what is the preferred name, rather than making assumptions. We can easily think that we are being friendly by referring to a young person by the 'nickname' peers use. In fact, we may unknowingly be colluding in putting the child down.

Supportive relationships and group work

Developing supportive relationships within a school follows on naturally from exploring the language we use with one another. Later in this book we will make the link between addressing bullying and developing effective teaching and learning practice in the school, but an initial question we could ask is: what opportunities do children have to work in groups, and when they do, how well do they do this? Do they work in a group, or as a group? Group work needs very careful management.

How have the groups been constructed? (Are they friendship groups, and if so does this mean they reinforce rather than challenge each other's opinions and values? How do you support the child with no friends in the class? How do you support such a child to 'break into' an established or strong friendship group?)

Do the groups reflect a balance of styles of team work? (Is there a natural leader/organiser, researcher, thinker, worker, etc.)

Does each member of the group have a clear role and task? (Or is one member of the group doing all the work, and hence most of the learning?)

In addition to processing the task, is the group asked to reflect on the way they worked? (Did they co-operate with each other, question each other, share the tasks?)

Simple ideas can help relationships. At the end of the first half term, one large secondary school uses the smallest individual school photographs of the children to create a display. Each child sticks a photograph in the middle of a sheet of paper, writes underneath, 'My name is... and my form thinks that I am...' and then draws 'clouds' around it. The class then circulate these sheets and each person writes something positive in the clouds. The teacher includes his or her own photograph and sheet and supervises the process. At the end, a huge display is put up under a heading of 'We are… and this is our class'.

Peer counselling

Many schools in both the primary and secondary phase have established systems of peer support. In primary schools personal links are made between older children and younger children ranging from simple joint reading activities that build relationships across the age range through to more complex peer counselling and even peer mediation schemes. It is not always easy for young children to approach their older peers. Systems that enable older students to be pro-active in enquiring about the welfare of their junior colleagues can help with this.

Older children in many primary schools share the responsibility of supervising the playground areas reserved for the very youngest pupils. In one school this task has to be applied for. Interviews are carried out by a panel of older, more experienced children. Would-be applicants are asked a range of questions relating to dealing with quarrels, bullying, inappropriately rough behaviour, lonely children and minor accidents. Even to get on the reserve list is considered to be an honour.

This is a small step in itself but it reinforces the school's determination that children shall feel safe, be protected from bullying and can recognise when over enthusiastic, over energetic behaviour becomes bullying, or appears as bullying.

Many secondary schools have found that linking new year 7 children with older children helps the settling in phase and also gives greater responsibility to the whole school community for the welfare and safety of students.

Westcliff High School for Girls operates a 'sisters and aunts' scheme. Year 7 children are linked with a year 8 'sister' for general support and a sixth form 'aunt' who can support more complex difficulties. Time for private contact is made available through

Some secondary schools adopt a 'guardian angel' scheme. Each new student is paired with an older student, without knowing who the older student actually is

tutorial sessions and a simple postal system. Peer support is not a substitute for staff driven pastoral systems but it enriches the range of support available to a young person, whilst sending a clear message that the wider school community cares.

Another simple system adopted by some secondary schools involves a 'guardian angel' scheme. Each new student is paired with an older student, without knowing who the older student actually is. They are allocated a number. If newcomers wish to write to their older 'angel' they address their letter with their 'angel's' number and post it in a special box. The older student knows both the writer's name and number. The 'angel' then either writes back with advice or takes appropriate action.

Because the 'angel' is not known, potential bullies never know if their potential victims are being watched. These schemes seem very complex and perhaps even a little unrealistic, but a number of schools report that they work well.

Whatever system a school adopts, training by staff or, if the system is established by older students, on-going staff supervision and support is always essential. Any member of a peer support structure needs to understand the boundaries within which they operate, have the skills to carry out their task and know when a referral to a staff member needs to be made.

The counselling and mediation skills that young people acquire through these schemes can have wide benefits to the young people themselves. Peer support can be a highly effective means of improving relationships within a school, but only as part of a whole school approach to behaviour management.

Safe and less safe locations

We have already looked at how the school could identify safe and less safe locations. Depending on the age of the children, the type of supervision that may be appropriate for areas defined as less safe will be different. With younger children, staff will need to increase their vigilance in these areas; for older children, the responsibility for this may be delegated to the children themselves.

Ambitious projects have been carried out by a number of primary schools to encourage the children to redesign the playground. This gives children opportunities to create their own play environment. One school in Essex realised that football games were dominating the playground, so children worked with a local architect to introduce simple playground zoning. This included moving

If the school's approach to addressing bullying is inconsistent, it really does undermine everyone's efforts and children will see through this

playground furniture, introducing picnic tables and raising one area very slightly with paving slabs to make a 'stage area'.

The school also had an unused 'quadrangle' that was opened to make a quiet reading area. This was supervised and ensured that any young person who felt uncomfortable in the larger playground had a place to go. The school was aware that a sanctuary was important but that it should only be a short term solution and not a 'prison' for children who actually would prefer to be in the playground. The supervising staff therefore made sure that they spoke with every child in this area to pick up any difficulties very quickly.

Another primary school involved the lunch time supervisors working with children in creating a large book of 'playground games'. During lunch time, supervisors helped to organise and run many of these games. This meant that children who might feel threatened or isolated could join in games, confident that an adult was ensuring their safety and inclusion.

Safe and unsafe times in the passage of the day
Some children very clearly identify some times of the day as being especially difficult. These have included:
- **Waiting outside a classroom for the teacher to arrive**
- **Travelling to and from school, especially just outside the school gates**
- **Lunch queues**
- **Changing rooms, especially if teacher supervision is weak**
- **Cloakroom areas at the beginning and end of the day**
- **Moving in and out of the building, especially if older students 'hang out' at the exits**
- **Any time the teacher leaves the class**

Once these have been identified, schools can explore strategies for tackling problems.

Inconsistent approaches to managing incidents
Children are quick to identify which teachers will respond sympathetically and constructively to requests for help. This can be a real problem. If a school does not have a consistent whole school policy, one or two members of staff can find themselves being the focus for more than their share of crises! While children will choose their own counsellors, and some teachers seem to radiate a certain 'something' that indicates they can be approached and will listen and help, having an agreed and consistent policy helps spread the load.

It is also worth remembering that in a real crisis, a young person's choice of counsellor can be very surprising. Any member of staff who is convinced that no young person will ever approach them for help may be in for a surprise.

One group of eleven year olds identified a 'fierce' teacher as an

The
supply teacher
won't
understand!

Supply teachers
should be briefed
on known
problems with
bullying

ideal choice if you were being bullied, because if you were being hurt you needed a 'really nasty person' on your side!

If the school's approach to addressing bullying is inconsistent, it really does undermine everyone's efforts and children will see through this. Sadly, only one or two incidents of inconsistent management of bullying incidents can undermine the credibility of all of your work, hence the need to involve all staff in development work.

Bullied children or children recovering from bullying can feel anxious if a supply teacher takes their class, especially in a primary school. Will they know what has been happening, will they know that an agreement has been reached that if the young person feels anxious, can he asked for help, etc? It is important to brief supply teachers about any known problems, agreements or contracts with bullied children or children who have bullied. A day with a supply teacher can easily seem like a 'different day', since children may feel that promises made to their teacher do not count.

SELF ESTEEM

We feel that self esteem is so important, we needed to give it a section of its own. There are many ways that we can explore self esteem. Without high self esteem, how do you:

- **Like yourself, believe yourself to be likeable or loveable?**
- **Enjoy life, school or learning?**
- **Assert yourself?**
- **Negotiate as an equal?**

- **Feel able to cope with, or at least minimise the effects of, difficult times in life?**
- **Contribute or participate as a full member of a team?**
- **Challenge others' views and accept challenges to our own?**
- **Cope with confrontation?**
- **Make changes?**

We think of self esteem as:

- **Our sense of self worth – the degree to which we value ourselves**
- **Our sense of self image – how we think others see us**
- **Our sense of self confidence – the energy we can draw upon when we need to assert ourselves or just feel in control**

If you think about your own self esteem, the chances are it is built up by three factors:

- **Activities that you feel you do well, or effectively**
- **Important activities or activities of value to you or to others**
- **Your achievements recognised or celebrated by you or by others**

As adults, we are often able to praise ourselves, but children thrive on the recognition and praise of significant adults and their peers.

If we want to build the self esteem of children, Bill Rice offers this model outlined in the TACADE resource *Skills for Adolescence*. He likens self esteem to a stool with three legs.

Building self esteem requires us:

- **To equip children with skills, help them to see how they can be applied and how to reflect on how successfully they were applied**
- **To give them what they see as real responsibility**
- **To demonstrate we appreciate their efforts**

He argues that all three must be in balance or self esteem wobbles or even collapses.

For example, if we acquire a new set of skills, but are never asked to apply them, we may doubt others share our belief in our ability. If we are given new responsibilities without the skills to carry them out, at best we feel anxious, at worse immobilised. If we are never praised for our efforts, we can find ourselves doubting the quality of our work.

Many people find their self esteem is built on a very narrow, although sometimes very high, set of factors. This can make us very vulnerable to a sudden change of circumstance. Perhaps one of the tasks of schools is to help children build their self esteem on as wide a foundation as possible. A number of children who bully others have

If we identify that many children who bully others have low self esteem, one positive strategy to try would be to increase the responsibilities of the bully

learning difficulties. This highlights the importance of the school celebrating children's achievements in both the academic and non-academic curriculum. This can be quite a challenge with some young people and it reinforces the need for teachers to really know their children well.

All this creates an interesting question: is the raising of everyone's self esteem a managed part of the life of your school? It is so easy simply to say that this is fundamental to the ethos of our school, but how do we actually ensure that this is happening?

If we identify that many children who bully others have low self esteem, one positive strategy to try would be to increase the responsibilities of the bully. We need to be honest with the child. They need to know that they have behaved as a bully and are guilty of unacceptable behaviour. We are giving her or him responsibility as a way of helping them to stop behaving in this way.

With some young people it can be really hard to find something that they can do really well or an interest that can be built upon. This may be a sign that the school needs to draw on external support from parents or other agencies.

This approach, if matched to the young persons skills and linked with appropriate praise can be highly effective in reducing the need to bully others. Some schools argue that this rewards the bully. We have found that other children are very tolerant of this approach and do not view it in this way, perhaps being glad that the school is attempting to address the problem. If we accept that the school has an equal responsibility for the education and welfare of every young person, and that this should acknowledge unequal starting points, a therapeutic approach to addressing bullying is appropriate.

If we are confronted by an incident of vicious bullying, we need to consider how the children involved have reached this moment. The degree of responsibility that a person who bullies has for his or her actions is philosophically beyond the scope of this book, but our premise is that we have a responsibility to stop the bullying and guide the children involved into more civilised behaviour.

Self discipline and external or imposed control are often confused. Discipline comes from within and is present even when the external control is absent. Control can appear highly effective up until the moment it can no longer be applied. In our approach to addressing bullying we need to work with children to ensure their behaviour is appropriate even when we are not present. If we only provide control, we do little to educate children who bully others.

There is a danger of making children feel that 'discipline' like 'health' or 'safety' are abstract concepts, the responsibility of 'others', 'people out there', 'people in authority'.

It might be worth wording your policy to use 'keeping safe', 'being healthy and keeping healthy' and 'being disciplined' as more personally relevant titles.

So the behaviour or discipline policy becomes:

● **Our being disciplined policy**
● **Our policy about the way we behave**

We need to take every opportunity and use every strategy to help children and young people understand that these concepts start and end with them and in them and not with people 'out there'.

SCHOOL SYSTEMS

Let us look at two practical examples of systems that primary and secondary schools have put in place.

Chelmer Valley High School in Essex adopted a simple mechanism for helping children report bullying that was happening to themselves or others.

Following discussion throughout the school and a review of the school equality of opportunity policy, three codes of practice were created by a working party. The first lists the approach to be adopted by staff if bullying is even suspected and a clear set of actions that are then required. The second protocol outlined the school's recommended action for children who are experiencing bullying. It makes it clear that the school finds this unacceptable, that it hurts everyone and that it is never justified. The third is a protocol for any young person who feels that another is experiencing bullying. This division is interesting since it enabled children for whom personal bullying was not and perhaps never had been a problem, to have a clear and separate requirement placed upon them to help others.

The school then placed a batch of report forms in every classroom for teachers to record incidents of actual or suspected bullying. This enabled a clear report of what was happening to be passed to senior management in order to intervene and for a record to be kept of the type of bullying, making it possible to monitor and

Are you being bullied?
If so:
Don't put up with bullying

DO - Tell an adult
DO - Tell your parents
DO - Write down what has happened
DO - Keep away from the source of the trouble

Have things improved?
If not:

DO - Start again
DON'T - Accept the situation

Help stop bullying by telling someone. It hurts everybody

quickly deal with trends in bullying behaviour, such as racism or sexism. The blank forms were also pinned to the form notice board rather than kept in a desk. This again reinforced the high profile being given to this issue. The following page illustrates their protocols.

An additional stage being piloted by another school is to provide children with a self reporting form. This can be completed by any young person who wishes to anonymously report that he or she is aware of or has have witnessed bullying. Once completed, forms are placed in a wooden letter box near, but not too near, the staff room. The location was chosen to enable the posting to be as private as practical in a busy school.

There was some concern that this extra system might be abused by children wishing to get their peers into trouble, but from the setting up of the system to date of publication of this book, this has not happened. This type of self reporting has advantages, since it helps to bypass the 'code of silence' that can exist in some schools, but arguably does little to break it down and if abused could set up something quite sinister or 'big brotherish'). Whilst this is worth reflecting upon, the system is helping teachers make the opening moves in support of some vulnerable children who do not feel able to ask for help. Perhaps this is a step along the road to a 'bully free school'.

One of the schools working with us is currently developing a process of creating what is turning out to be quite a simple code of conduct for children, but the process itself has involved virtually every young person in the school.

By using classroom discussion and draw and write activities, children explored what they felt is included in the words, 'good behaviour'. The first stage was then to draw these thoughts into clusters and then to reduce them to something that would be easy to read for older pupils, and something that could be discussed between parents and younger children. The school was committed to making a practical, living document that every young person, parent and member of staff would own.

The school was clear that they wanted the document to be as inclusive as possible, so references to 'teachers' and 'pupils' were replaced by 'we' and 'everyone', since the qualities that were identified were created by everyone and appropriate to everyone!

HOME SCHOOL CONTRACTS

A number of schools, especially secondary schools, are now introducing 'Home School Contracts' or agreements between parents, the school and in many cases the children. These clarify what are the responsibilities and entitlements of each party.

If you see someone being bullied

DO -   Tell an adult
DO -   Be kind and listen to the victim
DON'T -   Ignore bullying – it won't go away
DO -   Get the help of friends
DON'T -   Be provoked into taking the law
              into your own hands

NOBODY should have to put up with bullying

As with many activities such as this, Home School Contracts have real benefits. There is no doubt that they make a number of issues explicit. They help to clarify the process of making the education of children a partnership between the family, the young person and the school. But these contracts or agreements are not the solution to all problems with relationships. The main purpose of contracts should be to help prevent difficulties from arising, but placing demands on children must be balanced by ensuring they have the skills to enable them to meet their part of the contract.

The challenge to schools is how they manage the situation where the contract is in danger of or is being broken. One clear advantage is that it does offer the school an opportunity to engage in a dialogue with parents using the headings within a contract as a route into discussion.

The education of children is not a bargain that is struck between two parties, but a partnership involving many years of work. There is a world of difference between using a home school contract as a means of proportioning blame, or making demands, and using the contract as a vehicle for developing an agreed joint action plan that all parties feel able to enact. Parents and carers may need a lot of help with positive strategies, otherwise unco-ordinated or even conflicting strategies can make situations far worse!

Many contracts are put in place to encourage or promote good behaviour, to ensure homework is done on time and to ensure that when children are sanctioned, they know why this is happening.

The best contracts go far beyond this and link into the school's overall aims and may drive parts of its development plan. Contracts place a great responsibility on the school. Entering into a contract with the whole school community that states 'We will provide a safe environment for all our children' is quite a commitment!

STUDENT DIARIES

One useful idea that some teachers use is to give their students a diary. At some time in each day the student has some time to fill it in. This diary remains the confidential property of the student; however, a student who wishes to can give it to the teacher to read. This simple technique has proved very useful in a number of schools and could be used in both the primary and secondary phases. It is very important to help children keep their confidential diaries safe from other children's eyes.

One of our colleagues has an agreed code with his children. If any of them need his help, they just say 'Can you spare two minutes?' and at some time in the day he has guaranteed them two minutes of confidential time. Agreeing these types of mechanisms can make it easier to approach staff, since the opening has already been made. It also demonstrates that staff expect to be approached, and that this is okay.

CHAPTER FOUR

Address incidents of bullying

The majority of incidents of bullying behaviour occur in school or on the way to and from school. We have therefore decided to approach addressing incidents of bullying by looking at a number of incidents from the teachers perspective, beginning with the moment when the teacher has reason to be alarmed 'that something is going on'.

In real life, each incident needs to be considered as a unique event and it is not possible to offer a strategy that can be applied like a script to deal with every incident of bullying, but working through some situations might be helpful and many of the strategies and principles will remain the same.

Incidents of children harming one another are likely to come to light in a variety of ways. They can be:

● When a member of staff or other children witness an incident
● When a lunch time or mid-day assistant refers an incident to a teacher
● When a bullied child discloses this to a member of staff
● When a member of staff is approached by another child, perhaps a friend of the harmed child, who is aware of what is happening
● When incidental remarks are made through activities such as circle time
● When a complaint is made by an anxious parent

PART ONE: DISCOVERING THE INCIDENT

We will begin by looking at a number of situations, where it appears that bullying behaviour is discovered to be taking place. We will then consider possible strategies to move these situations forward.

The approach for help from a primary school child

Let's start with a typical primary school incident:

A six year old child tells you that another group of children are 'bullying her'.

The first problem is to find out exactly what the child means and what has happened. Asking a six year old child to accurately recount

---

It can be worth taking the child to the place where he or she thinks the bullying happened and helping to work through what occurred

---

what has happened, when and by whom is asking quite a lot. From our experience of working with very young children, their verbal accounts tend to be disjointed, events tend to get recounted out of sequence, the child is easily distracted and it is easy to let the whole incident pass by.

For young children, just telling an adult or being with a teacher may make them feel safe enough to temporarily dismiss or diminish the significance of what has previously happened. This doesn't mean the situation, whatever it was, won't happen again.

It can be worth taking the child to the place where he or she thinks the bullying happened and helping to work through what occurred. Another alternative is to ask the child and the alleged bullies to draw what each think happened and dictate in a whisper, if necessary, exactly what they think has occurred. One picture may not be enough to fully explore what young people are thinking. The adult and the child both look down at the drawing. This is easier than a face to face confrontation.

The adult's skill is in leading the child into telling what has happened. It can be simply, 'Is this you?...How are you feeling in your picture?... Who is this?' This can offer a route into discussing what went on, whether it was appropriate or not and how to behave towards one another in future.

With very young children, it can also be helpful to raise the subject of how we make others feel sad, lonely or upset. A powerful route into this is through stories. We cannot over emphasise the potential for using good children's literature as a route into bullying and virtually all other sensitive issues. We will return to this in our chapter on exploring issues of bullying as a curriculum issue.

With very young children, teachers can get a feeling that relationships are not as positive in their class as they would like. Using good children's stories is a powerful yet safe way of helping to explore issues around relationships.

Witnessing an incident with older children
Let us look at an example of an incident from the lower end of the secondary school:

A member of staff witnesses an incident of a small group of older children gathered around a younger child on a staircase. The younger child is in year 7 (the first year of an English secondary school), the older children are in year 9. It is towards the end of breaktime. The younger child is pushing one of the older children and seems about to punch one of the group. Some of the group are laughing, but two look very aggressive. A similar situation could be equally applicable to the top end of a primary school.

The first thing might be to find out what is happening, but there are two problems:

● **If this younger child is being intimidated by a group of older children, being surrounded by potential bullies, on a staircase**

'Don't let me ever catch you bullying again'

Does the teacher appear to be saying: 'Don't bully' or: 'Don't get caught bullying'?

with a lesson due to start at any moment and perhaps already feeling highly distressed, the victim is unlikely to be able to give a full account of what is currently happening and what may have been taking place let alone over a long period of time

● The next lesson is due to start at any minute and the teacher will have 30 unsupervised children waiting

The easiest thing might be to separate the bullied from the bullies, send them both off in different directions with a suitable comment aimed at all of the bullies such as:

'Don't let me ever catch you bullying again'

and a supportive comment to the bullied child such as:

'Off you go, and if anything like this happens again, tell your form tutor'

Actually the teacher may have communicated something quite different. To the bullies they may have communicated:

'I am assuming that this is a one-off incident, so if teachers do catch you again you are only likely to be disciplined for that event, not the term of systematic abuse that may have been happening'

'As a staff we don't take this sort of incident very seriously; certainly it is not as important as missing out on homework, or being late for school three times in a term, for which we give a school detention'

'It is okay to do this, just don't let me catch you!'

And to the bullied:

'Although I saw what was going on, I don't really have time to listen to you and to help. I have stopped this from going further today, now it is up to you to keep yourself safe'

'I am not really interested in what has been going on in your life up until now'

'If you are getting bullied a lot, you can't count on all the teachers to be ready to help you. Try your form tutor, it's their job!'

Instead of responding in one of these ways, perhaps the first thing to do is to gain some space. An incident such as this is important for everyone in that it needs to be dealt with properly and swiftly, but is not an emergency in that it needs to be resolved immediately. In this case the most urgent things to do are:

- **Reassure the pupil who seems to have been bullied that you take what has happened very seriously and that you will give support**
- **Separate the bullied child from the bully or bullies and in the short term offer the harmed a place of safety**
- **Fix times when everyone concerned can be seen, with the harmed young person being seen first**

> *It can be very easy to slip into a 'discipline voice' and use this same tone with everyone involved, including the harmed young person*

The language teachers use at his point is very important. It can be very easy to slip into a 'discipline voice' and use this same tone with everyone involved, including the harmed young person.

Since we know we are going to be setting up a counselling session with the harmed young person with either ourselves or a colleague our language at this stage is very important in setting the tone for our later work.

> *'I saw what was happening and you look really upset. Look, I have got another class waiting for me, but I think we really need to talk about this. Could we meet at…? So I will see you at…'*

is likely to be more productive than:

> *'I can't see you now, see me at 3.45 outside my office.'*

We also need to be careful how we address the bullies. If we are trying to make it clear that uncivilised behaviour is unacceptable, behaving in an uncivilised way towards the bullies gives the message that uncivilised behaviour is acceptable if you are in authority!

We have said that a place of safety should be offered in the short term. This is important as some schools, with the best of intentions, end up isolating or restricting the movements of the bullied young person rather than the bullies. Whilst a place where children can go who feel at risk is essential in a whole school approach to bullying behaviour, these places can end up as a long term refuge for some children. We are back to the notion of equality of opportunity. Every young person should be able to access the playground without fear of harm or abuse, so keep places of safety as short term measures for individual children.

THE ANXIOUS CHILD

Although many of the principles will remain the same, another way that we might discover that someone is being bullied is when we see a young person who is demonstrating that he or she needs to share something with us but may not have the skills or vocabulary to do so. Sometimes we may find ourselves knowing what to say, exactly what words to use, but when we open our mouths either the words won't come out or we say something totally different. Children will do this at any age.

One thing is certain: while schools can set up pastoral systems to provide counselling services, children will chose their own counsellors. No member of staff can 'opt out' of being seen as a potential counsellor, although some teachers may reject the approach or wish to refer it to another colleague. In primary schools we have found that support staff, school secretaries, adults helping in the classroom, mid-day supervisory staff, the school nurse, caretakers and cleaning staff have all been approached by worried children. Perhaps some children feel they have more control over disclosing to someone they see as a non-teacher staff member?

In secondary schools, a teacher may wish to refer to a year head or head of house. Any referral needs great sensitivity, since a referral can appear like a rejection to a young person who may have spent a considerable amount of time building up the confidence to approach a member of staff.

A member of the class has held back after a lesson or after school. We feel that there is something the child might want to talk to us about. For example, the child may be taking longer than usual to pack a bag and friends have left.

It can be quite hard to open up a conversation with children, especially if we may not feel we know them very well. We have to start from the assumptions

- **That they want us to begin a conversation and are at least prepared to meet us half way if we do**
- **That we have more developed interpersonal skills than they do, so opening this conversation is probably going to be down to us**

The first stage is to get the dialogue started. This may present a problem since children usually pick the worse possible moment to demonstrate that they need help. Unfortunately, a rejection now may mean that a young person does not seek help again, perhaps for some considerable time. By then things may be far worse.

It is important that you quickly cover four points:

1) **Acknowledge the need**
2) **Explain that the reason you cannot meet immediately is not because of a lack of care or interest**
3) **Confirm your wish to continue the contact**
4) **Get a commitment for you both to meet again**

If we are really pushed for time we may have to take a risk here. If the opening comment:

> *Something is worrying you, isn't it? Would it help to talk about it?*

is inappropriate, the worst that can happen is that the young person simply says that everything is okay and leaves. It is better to try this than let the moment pass.

If the response is that something is wrong, we need to set up a more appropriate time to continue the conversation.

INVITING A DIALOGUE

There are a vast number of opening lines that you can use to invite a dialogue.

It is important to again acknowledge that these children need help and to legitimise their need. They often need someone to say that it is not only all right to talk, but that what they want to talk about is important and that their thoughts, feelings and views are of value to you.

Openings can range from the general:

'How are things going?'

'How's life?'

'You were looking really worried earlier; would it help to talk about it?'

Children often need someone to say that it is not only all right to talk, but that what they want to talk about is important

To the more probing:

'You are not looking your normal happy/confident self; is there something wrong?'

'You were looking really worried earlier; would it help to talk about it?'

'Something is worrying you, isn't it? Can we talk it through together and see if I can do something to help?'
'How can I help?'

(But be careful with this one, it is not nearly as 'opening' as it first appears. The child may have no idea how you can help.)

Again we need to legitimise the need to talk:

'That would make me feel...'

'It can be really hard sometimes to...'

'I can understand why...'

'I can understand that feeling...'

can all be helpful to assist a young person to begin to talk.

GETTING PAST THE PRESENTING PROBLEM

Some children can offer what is known as a presenting problem. Young persons can present an opening problem either because the real problem is too sensitive and they need time to work up to talking about it or they need to test out our response to a 'low level' request for support, and will only go on to the real problem if we make them feel comfortable. We have to be careful here, because we may find ourselves assuming that the issue is a presenting problem, when actually it's not! Getting past a presenting problem must involve an invitation to talk more widely or deeply rather than an interrogation that puts the student off or appears to trivialise the initial problem. Try language such as:

'Is there anything else worrying you...?'

So we've sorted out that problem, then. Off you go...

Take care not to shut off a child's opportunity to talk about the problem that's really bothering them

'You still look a bit down ... is there something else you would like to talk about?'

'Okay, we have sorted out that problem, but you still look a bit down. How are things going generally?'

Or even:

'I know it can be really hard to talk about some things, but sometimes it helps and I need to know at least a little more if I am going to be able to help.'

Try to avoid:

'So everything is okay now, isn't it?'

'So we've sorted out that problem. Come and see me if there is anything else.'

Without wishing to overstate the issue, we often only get one chance at this. If we do not give young people an invitation to go further, using language that is open and shows genuine interest, they will either go elsewhere or nowhere.

If as a result of our conversation we uncover that a young person is being harmed then we need to begin the process outlined below.

NB: It may be that we discover that the young person is experiencing abuse that is covered by the local authorities' child protection procedures. If we even suspect that this is the situation, we must refer to the head teacher or the 'named person' within the school with responsibility for child protection, in order that these procedures may be followed.

THE CONCERNED PARENTS OR CARERS

Sometimes, in both primary and secondary education, it is the parents or carers of the young person who is being harmed who contact the school. It may be that they know the young person is being bullied or they may have noticed something else that is causing them alarm.

Building on Michele Elliot's (1992) list, any of the following signs may be indicators of being bullied:

- Being frightened of walking to or from school
- Being unwilling to go to school and making continual excuses to avoid going
- Begging to be taken or driven to school
- Changing the route to school every day
- Looking for excuses to stay in the school building at playtime
- Beginning to do poorly in school work
- Regularly having clothes, books or school work torn or destroyed
- Coming home starving (because dinner money or packed lunch was taken)
- Becoming withdrawn
- Starting to stammer
- Starting to act out or hit other children (as a reaction to being bullied by those children or others)
- Stopping eating or becoming obsessively clean (as a reaction to being called 'fatty' or 'dirty')
- Inventing illnesses at the time of setting off to school

- Developing stomach pains and headaches due to stress, or being sick just before going to school
- Attempting or threatening suicide
- Crying to sleep
- Beginning to wet the bed
- Having nightmares and calling out things like 'Leave me alone'.
- Having possessions go 'missing'
- Asking for money or beginning to steal goods or money (to pay a bully)
- Continually 'losing' pocket money
- Refusing to say what is wrong
- Bursting to go the toilet on arriving home (because of not being able to go all day)
- Giving improbable excuses to explain any of the above

Children may also arrive late for school or lessons, because of avoiding the playground or running into bullies. The child hangs around or hides outside school until everyone else has entered the building. We have also seen children avoid lining up outside a class to wait for a teacher, or hide until the teacher has arrived and entered the class. They fear any unsupervised situation.

We will now need to talk to the young person whom we fear may be being harmed. It is likely that we will need a similar dialogue to the one outlined earlier. Before we do this however, we might need to do some more checking out.

If we only have a letter from the parents or carers, we may wish to invite them into the school to talk through in more detail what they believe has been going on. We may get clear evidence that the young person is being harmed, or only hints and clues that there is some underlying problem.

We need to ensure that the parents know we are taking the matter very seriously and that we will inform them of our investigations and action. It is important to be clear in our own minds where the parents have control, in contacting the police for example, should the uncovered incident warrant such action, and the areas in which we have control, such as our own school discipline.

Beware of comments like:

'I want that bunch of bullies suspended or expelled'

The feelings and concerns of the carers must be acknowledged, while not necessarily agreeing to their demands.

'I appreciate how you must be feeling. We take this type of incident very seriously. Let us investigate what has been happening and we will get back to you as quickly as we can'

may be safer than:

'We take bullying very seriously in this school, and rest assured they will be dealt with most severely'

because a parent may assume that you just agreed with them, and at the moment you really do not know what is going on!

Another problem that teachers have reported is the parent who says:

'I have told him/her, if they try to hit you, you hit them back as hard as you can and I will back my child all the way'

Bear in mind that this is probably a very anxious and concerned parent who desperately wants to do something constructive. It is easy for the next part of the conversation to become confrontational.

It is essential to acknowledge how the parent is feeling. The child

Look – just hit them back as hard as you can!

Many children who are being bullied are unable to lash out. Hitting someone is not in their nature and this should be something we applaud

is having a rotten time, may be being hurt and may be very upset at home. As someone who wants to protect the child and to whom the child may be appealing for help, the parent is probably feeling pretty helpless and desperate. It is not surprising that a lot of anger is likely to be brought to the school by the parent.

We need to do two things and the first is to buy the school some time:

'We need some time to sort this out. I will give you a ring by the end of today/tomorrow morning and let you know what I have uncovered and what we will do'

We also need to make it clear that while hitting back might just work, it could equally make things ten time worse. The theory that all bullies are cowards, and one hard thump will make them go away, is naive. As a school you cannot agree to this approach (you might find you have agreed to someone suffering a serious injury!) and the school may end up having to sanction the victim, who currently seems to have enough problems.

Perhaps we need to say that we want children to be assertive, to stand up for themselves, but that aggression usually causes more aggression.

Parents can also misunderstand that telling a young person to hit someone is very different from actually doing it. Many children who are being bullied are unable to lash out. Hitting someone is not in their nature and this should be something we applaud. Sadly, the child who finally snaps and does lash out may use considerable force and cause a serious injury.

Any parents of bullied children who themselves threaten one of your pupils with violence have to be told that the school cannot allow this to happen. Every young person in the school is in the school's care and a threat to hurt a suspected bully should always be referred to the police.

PART TWO: UNPACKING AN INCIDENT AND MOVING FORWARD

We will now make the assumption that the teacher who has uncovered the problem is going to continue to work through what has happened and try to resolve what is going on.

In a primary school, it is likely to be up to the individual class teacher to move the issue forward. However, it is a good idea for primary teachers to share their concerns and strategies with their colleagues, since the bullying might not be restricted to one class.

In many secondary schools the policy would now be for the teacher to alert the form tutor or a member of the pastoral staff who would then take the investigation forward. However the school chooses to manage the next stage, the issues are broadly similar.

The teacher is going to have to 'unpack' what is going on and to do this we have to consider every person involved as an individual. Ideally we need to avoid the situation where the teacher is seeing one bullied child on his or her own and the group of bullies in their group. Whilst this is demanding on time, members of the group, especially more reluctant members, may be less likely to talk honestly and openly about what is happening if their peers are present, especially if they are also frightened of some of them.

So we need to establish:

● **Who was doing the actual abuse or harming?**
● **Who were the 'hangers on'? (Those who watch and support the harmers but don't actually assault the harmed person.)**
● **Who did what to whom?**
● **Although one or two people may have done the actual harming, who was the initiator of the bullying behaviour and are they 'hidden in the background'?**
● **How long has this been happening?**
● **When and where have other incidents occurred and what happened?**
● **Was anyone else involved?**

We might not be unpacking a clear case of bullying. We might be tackling an incident of suspected bullying, with no obvious victim, no obvious bully, no witnesses but just half-seen incidents or whispers that all is not well. We might be unpacking an incident of bullying that has been going on for some time and that the whole class knew about but feared speaking out.

One possible approach to either of these situations might be for the whole class to use the above headings as a confidential draw and write activity. Not only would this gather a considerable amount of information but could act as a stimulus for discussion about the responsibilities of the whole group. This would need to be handled very gently and sensitively!

The first interview with any bullied young person will also need very sensitive handling and may take a little time. This may be the first time this young person has had the opportunity to talk about a long period of systematic abuse. If this is the case, we must not assume that he or she is necessarily going to be able to give us a full and accurate account of everything that has happened without a lot of coaxing and support.

It is important to remember that the ability to recall in sequence is one which is acquired quite slowly. Many children, especially if emotionally stressed, will start with the most damaging part of the story and being pressed to start with what happened first…next… etc, can be damaging. As adults we need to listen to the child and then, through careful checking out, work with the child to construct the sequence of events.

Once you start this process younger children may also assume that you know more than you actually do. So:

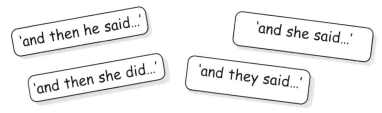

will need some careful checking out to make sure that you know who he, she and they are.

This is going to be particularly true if the incident has been referred to a member of staff with whom the young person has not established a relationship. For example, a year 7 student may only see a head of house or head of year as the person who takes assembly and sorts out discipline and sports fixtures and may be reluctant to talk about traumatic or painful events to someone not known well.

If we feel anxious or threatened, it can be difficult not to increase that feeling of vulnerability, even with someone we trust. Children (or their parents or carers) who are feeling threatened can respond in a variety of ways:

Denial	**The vulnerable child tries to deny the situation exists.**
Diversion	**The person tries to change the subject or keeps steering the conversation away from the issue.**
Aggression	**The child gets angry and may even run away.**

Withdrawal   The child becomes silent and seems unable or
                unwilling to co-operate.

Agreeing to   The child simply agrees to everything,
anything   hoping that the threatening
and   meeting will be over
everything   as quickly as possible.

Much will depend on the relationship between the child and the teacher. The degree of power children feel they have, their degree of control over what will happen and the degree of linguistic skills they possess will all play a part in how able they are to enter into a discussion about what has happened.

There is an issue of confidentiality and trust here. The teacher needs the facts about what is happening, because without these it is going to be very hard to move forward. The young person needs to feel sufficient trust in the teacher to be able to make a full disclosure of everything that has been going on, confident that the teacher will successfully resolve the problem by stopping any further abuse.

For young bullied persons, the risks are now very high. If they do not make a disclosure, things are likely to continue as they are and they may feel the teacher will not listen sympathetically next time. If they do make a complete disclosure and the bullies are not appropriately dealt with, there is a potential for the problem to get very much worse. For example, if the school's only response is to place the entire group of bullies in detention and then consider the incident closed the bullied may have a justifiable concern for their own future safety.

It is also possible that the bullies have required the harmed child to do things to which he or she will not want to admit. For example:

- **The young bullied child may have been forced to join in another episode of bullying**
- **The bullies may have demanded money, so the young person has stolen, perhaps from home**
- **The bullies may have demanded goods, so the young person may have been 'shoplifting'**

Some harmed children may already have very low expectations about what the teacher can do, in which case the details they may wish to go into might be very limited.

'It's okay, they were just mucking about. There's nothing really going on...'

As we have said earlier, this is sometimes known as a presenting statement and it is very easy to accept it at face value and let the matter drop.

Other children might have very high, perhaps even unrealistic expectations, of what the teacher can do. They might give a very full account of all that has been happening in the sure knowledge that now this disclosure has been made the teacher will immediately make sure that nothing abusive ever happens again. (For example, the bully will be kept indoors, perhaps standing outside the headteacher's room at breaks and mid-day until further notice, or that the bully will be suspended or even expelled.) Unfortunately, this may not be possible.

The reality may be that the teacher, in the short term, can ensure that further incidents carry consequences for the bullies and try to ensure the harmed child has a place of safety, but cannot guarantee total safety. (It is a little like the police being unable to guarantee to protect property, but guaranteeing that they will investigate and prosecute offenders after the crime.) The teachers can also guarantee to regularly check with all parties involved to see what has been happening since the incident has been discovered.

ACTIVE LISTENING

If we are going to successfully unpack what has been happening, we are going to have to listen, and listening is a skill that needs considerable practice.

Listening involves using:

● **Our ears to hear what is said**
● **Our minds to listen to what the person is saying and not saying – and make sense of it**
● **Our mouths to offer feedback and encouragement**
● **Our body language to show interest.**

In any situation like this we need to consider:

Time **Do we have sufficient time to make sure the young person does not feel rushed? (Try not to look at watches every two minutes)**

Silence **Silence is one of our great cultural problems. We often find it hard to cope with silences from the person we are listening to and so we rush to fill the silence with our speech. We all need time to think especially if what we want to say is painful or even embarrassing. We need time to find an acceptable way of communicating and this takes time. It can be helpful to count to nine. If the young person has not responded try asking the question in a different way**

Place **We need a place to talk that is away from noisy corridors, or a place where the child's peers can't watch or overhear what is being said. Sadly, many teachers feel reluctant, for their own safety, to see a single child alone in a closed room or office. With imagination and sensitivity a place can usually be found that offers** appropriate privacy, without making the teacher feel vulnerable. If the teacher is concerned, it is always worth letting a senior colleague know that the interview is going to take place.

If a school is serious about supporting children, creating locations for private yet safe sensitive dialogues is essential.

Room setting This needs to be 'felt'. Sometimes talking across a table feels right, sometimes you will want to arrange for two chairs to just be placed near one another. Chairs facing one another is usually not a good idea and many people prefer a 'L' shape with one chair at 90 degrees to the other. This allows eye contact when we want it and for eye contact to be dropped naturally when we don't

Eye contact Again, this is a matter of feeling what is right. As a general rule, people who are feeling anxious seem to feel more comfortable if they are looked at whilst they are being listened to, but not when they are listening

Eye level We need to encourage this young person to feel empowered, so towering over them or looking down at them is not really appropriate. We need to place our eye level at about equal heights, if not placing our eyes even slightly lower than the child's. When working with younger children the authors tend to place the child on a stool or low chair and then sit on the floor. This lowering of status can be very helpful to a young person who is finding it very hard to open up about a difficult issue. It is also important with young children to make sure that you neither crowd them, nor sit so far away as to appear disinterested

Language We need to be very sensitive in what we say to a young person at the start of this session. Saying: *'Right, I want to know everything that has*

been going on' doesn't help either the child or
the teacher

It is important to ask open-ended questions, but it might also be
worth making some more personal contact.

*'Look, I saw what was going-on on the stairs and I was
really frightened for you. What is happening?'*

Consider some open-ended questions that are not focused, for
example:

*'Can you tell me a little more about what has been
happening?'*

'How do you feel about all this?'

Provide feed back into comments. This demonstrates you are
listening and also helps you to check out that you are hearing things
correctly, for example:

'So when you said... happened, you felt...'

It is also important to offer encouragement and validation of the
young person's comments. We need to remember that many
incidents of name calling, tripping or pushing can seem
embarrassingly trivial when described coldly to someone else.
(Telling someone that you were stared at by someone on a train late
at night can seem silly the following morning, but can be terrifying
at the time.)

*I can understand why you felt like you did; I would have
been upset if that had happened to me.*

Check to see if anyone else is being harmed. You may find that others are also experiencing similar problems but have not come forward for help.

Establish what the young person wants to happen next, in order to clarify any unrealistic expectations and agree what we as teachers will do next. At this point we need to be as clear as possible about what will happen next.

Ideally we now need to write down exactly what we have been told has happened and when. We need this account, checked out with the young person, because we will need to confront the bullies with an account of what, in the opinion of the harmed young person, has been happening.

We now need to make it clear to the young harmed person that his or her account is going to be put to the bullies and that we will let them know what happens. We must also ensure that the harmed child understands that any action or punishment will be the responsibility of the school.

BULLYING AND THE LAW

Now we need to look very carefully at what has been happening to see just how serious the abuse or assaults have been. We need to consider an important issue. Whilst there is no crime of bullying, physical assault certainly is a crime. Just because it has happened in school really makes no difference, it is still a crime.

Many children may be unaware that just the threat of physical injury is also a crime. A comment such as:

is illegal. The action that the police will take will depend on exactly what has been done and said, and also depends on the age of the children involved.

At this point we need to consider the possibility that we need to talk to the parents of the harmed child although it may be worth waiting until we have talked to the bullies. If it transpires that the young person has suffered physical assault, the parents may wish to contact the police and prosecute the bullies. The school should support such an action if this is the parents' wish. Eric Jones (1992) reminds that the vast majority of parents will want to leave the matter to the school, and if this is their choice they must trust the school to resolve the problem in the way it thinks appropriate.

If, as a result of our investigation, we uncover that the bullies have been abusing or assaulting the harmed child outside of school, or that others, perhaps older siblings unconnected with the school, are involved then this is a matter for the police and our role essentially becomes one of support.

This is one of the incidents where the school needs to be clear about the boundaries of its responsibility. The school may wish to help the parents make that initial police contact, perhaps through setting up a meeting with the school's police liaison officer.

CONFRONTING THE BULLIES

We now need to present our findings to the bullies to get their perspective. This is where it can be both useful for the teacher and powerful for the bullies to see that the incident has been recorded in writing. If we have a group of children who have been abusing or assaulting a child, it is possible that we have one or two central figures and perhaps some 'hangers on'.

Don't forget that the bullies may now be feeling vulnerable and may therefore exhibit the same behaviour of denial, diversion, anger, withdrawal, or 'agreement to anything' we outlined earlier.

Michele Elliot argues that there are no 'bystanders' in bullying. Children need to understand that there are:

- Those who harm
- Those who try to help, either by intervening or by telling someone else
- Those who ignore what is happening, and therefore allow it to continue

When we talk to our potential bullies we need to be clear what answers we find unacceptable. Eric Jones (1992) offers a series of excuses from bullies who have been confronted by their behaviour and suggestions of appropriate responses.

These are responses that we have gathered through workshop sessions with staff and mirror many of his observations and strategies. We asked staff to brainstorm the excuses they had been given for bullying. We then shared these out in small groups and asked staff to think about a response that would challenge the excuse in an assertive, but not aggressive fashion.

I was there but I didn't hurt him

Okay, you say you didn't do anything, but you could see the other person was distressed, why didn't you stop what was going on, or if you were afraid to do so, why didn't you tell someone?

Fun for whom? If a joke is a good one everyone laughs. A joke or act of fun that frightens another person is unacceptable and must stop.

It doesn't matter, the threat of violence is unacceptable and may even be a criminal action. Are you aware that the bullied child's parents may wish to contact the police? The victim would have to be a mind reader to know 'you didn't mean it'. He or she only heard what you said.

a victim is sad
a victim nice
a victim is someone
hoo is hirt
hurt

If we cause an accident, we usually say 'sorry' and try to help the person we have hurt or inconvenienced. We do not have the same accident with the same person on a number of separate occasions.

If we play a game then everyone agrees to join in. A game where everyone is a player and one person is the ball is unacceptable.

You may have been playing, but someone has been hurt. If we all are playing, we should all be having fun, and one of us is now very upset. This isn't playing.

The victim Tould the dina lade

Borrowing something means you had their permission and were intending to give it back. Actually you stole it. Let's talk about what really happened.

He gave it to us, it was his choice

Yes, he gave it to you after you threatened him. What choice did he really have?.

'GETTING REAL'

We need to 'get real'. The bullies need to be confronted with what is really happening and not be permitted to hide behind an 'acceptable excuse' or 'explanation'. They must understand that this type of response will simply not be accepted.

In some incidents we may feel that a young person has genuinely misunderstood what has been intended, or that the older child or children genuinely did not have any real malice in mind. In this case we need to ensure that they fully understand how their actions have been taken by the other child, who regardless of intention has been harmed. We need to remind these children that we have recorded the incident and that there must be no repetition and that they should learn from the incident.

Regardless of the bullies' 'reasons' or 'excuses' for the harming behaviour, it is the effect on the harmed young person that concerns us as teachers and the consequences of that behaviour that we are reacting to and will react to.

At this point, the school may wish to set some form of sanction, but it is essential that this is in proportion to the incident. It needs to be firm enough to make the point that this behaviour is not acceptable, will not be tolerated and carries consequences but not so extreme as to become a form of institutional bullying. If some children harm others because of low self esteem, making their punishment overly public can serve to make them feel important, even if it is in a negative fashion. Many schools try to make a sanction as positive or constructive as possible.

Most important is to set up some ground rules about future behaviour and about no further contact between the abusers and the abused until such time as the victim feels secure.

Some schools bring the bullied person together with the bully or bullies in order to work through what has happened and agree together how to move forward. This needs very careful consideration. Sadly, a productive and even cordial meeting between the bullied child and the bullies in the presence of a teacher (or even parents) is not always reflected in a subsequent unsupervised encounter.

Another strategy that has proved effective in some schools, especially with early incidents of bullying, is to require and enable the bully to apologise and make recompense to their victim. This can be in the form of a letter, a verbal apology or even a gift. This again needs very careful handling and should be negotiated with the victim.

The bullies need to know that the incident has been recorded and that we will be regularly checking with the harmed child to see that no further incidents take place. It can be helpful for the bully to see, read or have read to him or her what is in the report or record of the events. It helps if the bully reads or has read to him or her the school rules or contract regarding behaviour and identifies which rules have been broken.

We need to ensure that the bullies are given clear and firm guidelines about the school's expectations of them and how they will need to behave if they are to avoid any further possibility of being thought of as bullies. We also need to be very clear about what will be the consequences of a further incident. For example:

- **A more serious loss of privileges/free time**
- **Parents may be asked to come to the school**
- **The school may wish to suspend the pupil**
- **The police may need to become involved**

We then need to let the harmed child know what has been agreed and then carry out our agreement! It is very easy to let the checking-up stage slip, in which case the school's credibility both as a source of support and as a source of discipline is severely damaged.

Many schools have found that making a contract with the young person or people who have been bullying can be helpful. This helps set targets for more constructive behaviour that can be regularly checked by tutors.

It would be appropriate for the class teacher, tutor or year head to briefly talk with both the bullied child and the bullies on a daily basis for some time following the incident to monitor progress. (This should either be at different times of the day or involve two staff. We discovered one incident that a school had thought satisfactorily resolved, only to find that the bully had been intimidating the bullied child each evening when they both had to wait outside the same classroom for their 'check in'!)

We need to push a little beyond simply asking a young victim of bullying: 'Is everything is all right now? Has the bullying stopped?'

Most children will probably say 'yes'. Find out what happens now at the time when the bullying used to happen. For example, what are they doing at break time or how are they finding coming to school? The bullying may have stopped, but if they are hiding in a toilet all break, or behind a building because they are still too frightened to come out, we need to know.

The bullying may also actually have or be imagined to have changed. 'They don't hit me any more, but they keep on looking at me.' Rebuilding confidence in a young person who has been bullied can take some time.

This is where activities such as adult-led playground games at break or lunch time can really help re-integrate a young child who has feared the playground in the past. Children can also work on their own targets and record their achievements.

Equally, how is the bully now behaving? Do we have a young person who has no real friends and is really very isolated? If the bullying is now passed, is there another situation that needs to be worked on? For example, do we need to build up the self esteem of this young person?

'NO BLAME' APPROACHES TO BULLYING

Many schools now adopt a 'no blame' approach to bullying. This places the emphasis for supporting young people who bully through pastoral support and clear, monitored, target setting for future behaviour. This is not 'soft' approach to bullying, especially if your goal is to promote social behaviour rather than extract revenge. The starting point for the school is that the bully is in need of help rather than punishment and that the actions the school takes focuses on helping the young person achieve better behaviour. A 'no blame' approach sets the tone for the school's action.

For example, consider a young person who appears to misunderstand normal approaches by their peers as a physical attack and hits out. They may be encouraged through a series of targets to eventually be able to:

- **Stop**
- **Take a deep breath**
- **Think about how they are feeling**
- **Think about what has really happened**
- **Think about all the possible ways to react**
- **Think about what will happen next in each case**
- **Decide which is best for everyone**
- **Do it!**

Just getting the young person to 'stop and think' may be a major achievement!

There are real advantages to adopting a 'no blame' approach. It sends a message that all young people are valued and that young people who bully are in need of support and help. This may enable young people who witness or experience bullying to ask for help more quickly, knowing that when they do the bully will receive help rather than simply punishment. If a young person believes the bully will only be punished, there may be a very real fear that the bully or their friends will extract revenge later on, perhaps even far away from the school.

A 'no blame' approach does not mean that the young person who has been bullying should not be required to confront what has happened, how they felt, how their victims felt and what the consequences of their actions have been. It does not mean they need not make amends, nor does it mean that they may not be temporarily be isolated for the safety of other children.

A 'no blame' approach to bullying also does not mean that if targets for future behaviour are not met, the school may not resort to sanctions, for example a loss of privileges. The focus of the

Every child has a right to feel safe in school

dialogue, however, would be to explore why they were not met and how the young person could try a different approach, rather than the loss of the privilege. Privileges should always be swiftly reinstated when targets are achieved.

There is a danger that good social behaviour is simply expected in a school. There is nothing wrong with praising children who have met their targets for positively changing their behaviour. Depending on the circumstances that have brought them to bullying and their previous image of themselves within their peer group, this may be one of their greatest achievements.

This approach is not going to work for every young person, but if the school has tried this approach and failed, it is a powerful indicator that the school needs to seek support from another agency.

As in health promotion of any kind, no single approach works for every young person or in every situation. What we do know is a series of approaches, coming together bound by the same philosophy, that every child has a right to feel safe in school.

WHAT ABOUT THE REGULAR BULLIES?

Some children will be quite shocked that their behaviour is seen by the school as bullying and is treated as such. They may not have really thought through how their behaviour is being perceived by others and will quickly stop once the school has drawn their attention to how seriously it takes their behaviour.

Aggressive bullies whose behaviour, no matter what steps the school takes, makes them an ongoing threat to others; anxious bullies who deliberately attack older and stronger peers in order to seek attention or be bullied back; and children who bully others because they have suffered long-term abuse themselves, may all be beyond the physical resources and expertise of the school.

Persistent bullies need expert help and their backgrounds can be both complex and traumatic. Just as neither we as teachers nor the bullies themselves were responsible for their past history, so we cannot take on sole responsibility for the complex and multi-agency support they or their families may need.

If we are addressing a more persistent bully, we may need to draw on outside help such as the educational psychology service. It may become the case that another agency will take the lead, either in counselling, therapy or setting an action plan for modifying the behaviour.

If this happens, the teacher may move from being the lead professional to being in a supporting role. This will happen at different times in each individual school and will reflect the expertise of the staff.

We have to draw the line when addressing the needs of one young person is drawing so heavily on the resources of the school that other children are being disadvantaged.

The line must also be drawn when it becomes clear that the needs of the bully are beyond the resources of the school and that, if unchecked, their behaviour is likely to lead to other actions that could further damage their present and future lives.

CHAPTER FIVE

Build a curriculum

We need to build a programme of work that addresses bullying before bullying incidents happen. The problem is that if, as Kolb suggests, 'learning' involves activity, reflection, drawing out meaning and planning how to use this in future action, bullying others and being bullied is in itself a powerful learning experience. Creating learning situations in the classroom that will stop bullying on their own is unlikely. Once bullying is taking place we still need swift intervention.

Learning takes place at a variety of levels. We could think of learning experiences where:

- **The outcomes of the learning contribute to exploring or reducing bullying by, for example, exploring how a bullied character in a book might feel or react**
- **The process of learning contributes to reducing bullying – for example, activities that promote sharing, co-operation, taking turns and team-building**

If we are to help children explore deep learning, such at their personal beliefs and values, rather than shallow learning, such as a transmission of knowledge, we need an appropriate teaching methodology. Chris Watkins et al (1996) suggest that when teachers plan for effective learning, the tasks and processes need to promote:

- **Active learning**
- **Collaborative learning**
- **Learner responsibility**
- **Learning about learning**

If 'learning' involves activity, reflection, drawing

out meaning and planning how to use this in

future action, bullying others and being bullied is

in itself a powerful learning experience

There is an elegant argument here, since the activities that are likely to improve relationships and self esteem in the classroom, and hence reduce bullying, are also central to creating a classroom within which effective learning can take place. Building individual self esteem and positive working relations are central to improving the academic curriculum rather than peripheral to it.

If we are to help children explore their feelings, emotions, beliefs and values, we need an appropriate classroom climate that enables children to expose those feelings, to feel comfortable when they are challenged and to have the self esteem to feel able to modify those beliefs in the light of this challenge. We have discussed the creation of ground rules elsewhere, but the relationship between the teacher and the learners, the way groups are managed, the degree to which language used in class is inclusive and positive, and the way children are listened to will all facilitate or impoverish effective learning. In our day-to-day practice, we need to use positive teaching strategies across the curriculum and to reward all kinds of positive behaviours.

GETTING STARTED!

At this stage we should be asking ourselves how and if we can build a curriculum which aims to make our schools places where bullying is not tolerated. This means a curriculum which enables the pupils:

1) To recognise what bullying is and what it can be
2) To understand how it feels to be bullied, whether physical or psychological, whether it is something which could be thought of

as gentle teasing or something which is severe enough to warrant outside intervention
3) To understand what can lead children to bully others, whether it is a lack of awareness of the damage which it incurs or whether it is deliberate
4) To know how to deal with incidents of bullying, whether they are victims or not, to know how to tell the right person and to use the right words, those which alert adults in authority to the problem

What kind of curriculum is implied if these are some of our aims, and where does the school's bullying policy fit into this?

We would say that every school needs a policy for ensuring that bullying, if it happens, does not go undetected, but such a policy is not a curriculum. If a school is truly committed to being intolerant of any kind of bullying behaviour, it will have a planned programme with its aims clearly set out, some way of regularly identifying needs (since needs are constantly changing) teaching methodologies and evaluation strategies which enable the children to participate and review.

A spiral programme is needed, one which begins with the youngest children, those who are just leaving babyhood behind, and moves through their school lives, from the threshold of adolescence to the threshold of adulthood.

At each stage of that spiral there needs to be a programme:

● Where the content and the information are appropriate
● The language is appropriate
● The activity and teaching methodology are suitable

Each time the topic is revisited the programme has to demonstrate that:

● The content and language are becoming more specific
● The activity and teaching methodology are more challenging and demanding

Such a programme will always build on previous:

- **Understanding**
- **Language**
- **Content**

and will be very different from a programme motivated by bullying incidents.

If such a programme is going to succeed then it will have to offer teachers a strategy for identifying the needs of the children, and also enable teacher and class to monitor and evaluate their own learning and perhaps rethink the programme itself.

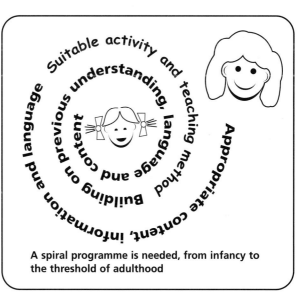

A spiral programme is needed, from infancy to the threshold of adulthood

We offered a research tool in chapter two, but in a primary school you might like to try something less formal. Try something like this:

Draw someone teasing a kitten.

What is your person doing?

Does the kitten like being teased?

What will the kitten do to show it doesn't want to be teased any more?

Repeat this, changing the kitten for a child, a friend, a little child or any other character.

Draw a bully.

How can we tell from your picture that this is a bully?

Draw what the bully is doing.

Why do you think the bully is doing this now?

Draw someone who has been bullied

How does this person feel?

What is this person doing?

Why did this person get bullied?

You could follow this work up with:

Put yourself in the picture.

What are you saying to the person?

Use what the children tell you to plan your class or school policy. You could also use these openings as an evaluation technique.

A SPIRAL OF SKILLS

Alongside the spiral of content, language and teaching methodologies, there needs to be a spiral of skills. Without these skills the programme is incomplete and likely to become just another lesson.

The skills and competencies that children and young people need in order to be active in ensuring that their school does not tolerate bullying are those of:

- **Confidence and self esteem**
- **Empathy; the ability to see and feel another person's situation**
- **Ability to relate behaviour to outcomes**
- **Ability to see alternative solutions**
- **Ability to recognise critical moments in extreme situations**
- **Ability and motivation to speak up; to be able to make an adult listen and to insist on being heard**
- **A language of emotions**
- **The ability to recognise one's own feelings and to know when to use that knowledge and when not to let it take control**
- **Ability to reflect on all this and to learn from that reflection**

Try this task. It is suitable for teachers, parents, governors and older pupils. It is suitable for all phases.

Ask the group working together or in smaller consortia to respond on paper, or with you as a scribe, to the following task:

Think about a 16 year old girl or boy, either just about to leave school or to move from school to college.

What would you want that 16 year old to:

- **Know and understand**
- **Feel about themselves and others**
- **Be able to say**
- **Be able to do**

about bullying, being bullied, when faced with bullying or hearing reports of bullying?

The chart on pages 98-99 brings together some of the responses we have had from just such a group.

Responses to bullying

KNOW	UNDERSTAND
● That some behaviours are acceptable and that others are not	● How we can 'feel hurt' – physically and emotionally
● That some people are responsible for keeping us safe	● That others can 'feel hurt' and be able to empathise with their feelings
● That we have a responsibility for keeping ourselves and others safe	● What 'feeling safe' means
● That feeling uncomfortable, hurt, anxious or scared needs talking about	● What 'taking risks' means
● Where to get help, who to ask for help and what the response will be	● Sharing and turn-taking
● A vocabulary of their feelings	● Their feelings and emotions and how others might exhibit their own feelings
● How to use assertive language without aggression	● They and others have equal rights and responsibilities
● How to negotiate a compromise	● The meaning of stereotyping and its dangers
● That not every disagreement is an incident of bullying	● That doing nothing can sometimes be wrong
● That some places are safe and that others are less safe	● That there are good and bad secrets, and that no-one has the right to insist you keep a bad secret
	● Which behaviours are appropriate or inappropriate within a friendship
	● That actions have consequences
	● That others have valid viewpoints, but that doesn't mean we have to surrender our viewpoint
	● How to work constructively in a group
	● Their own strengths when working in a team
	● That not all situations can be quickly solved

FEEL	BE ABLE TO SAY	BE ABLE TO DO
• A high degree of self esteem	• 'No'	• Make choices
• Included, able to participate and able to influence decisions	• 'Stop'	• Make judgements based on information
	• 'I'll tell'	• Listen to others
	• 'I'll ask'	• Offer viewpoints and counterpoints
• Valued	• 'Please help me'	• Work collaboratively as part of a group
• Skilled	• 'Please help my friend'	
• Successful	• 'Please help that person'	• Walk away
• Empathy for others	• 'I am feeling...' and have language that enables this to be communicated clearly to others	• Escape from an attack
• Respect for one another		• Get help and work with that help through an agreed strategy
• Confident to act in support of others		• Confront and work through issues in a controlled and safe environment
• A sense of justice or fairness		• Handle aggression and confrontation
• Able to let go of a relationship if it is inappropriate		• Manage anger and frustration constructively
		• Manage fear constructively
		• Cope with sudden or unwanted change

When the group has completed this part of the task, ask them to go through their lists and delete anything which would not be appropriate for 11 year olds.

If the group is primary phase, or as an example to secondary phase people of the importance of a spiral approach to an anti-bullying programme, ask them to repeat the activity deleting:

- **Anything inappropriate for seven year olds**
- **Anything inappropriate for four year olds**

We are certain that very little will be deleted. Your group will come quickly or not so quickly to the conclusion that every aspect can be introduced to the youngest children, provided it is done in a positive, relevant way with appropriate language.

You will now have a relevant starting point for planning your programme in a truly spiral way.

The PSE Curriculum

How are we to achieve this in today's already overcrowded curriculum? We can incorporate it as an ongoing strand in our health education or PSE programme. We know it will have to take its place among the many other topics and issues (ever increasing) which weave together to form these programmes. Before deciding that there isn't room for one more topic or that bullying will have to take its place along with drugs, healthy eating, dental health, sex education, personal hygiene and personal safety, look at the chart again. How many of the entries in the five columns are related to at least one other topic than bullying?

The English Curriculum

Another area of the curriculum where bullying and being bullied can be tackled is in the English programme. In return, the topic itself can provide a relevant context for developing many skills. They will include those of listening, speaking, reading, writing skills, skills of presenting a case, taking part in a debate, planning and evaluating a campaign, public speaking and writing reports, newspaper articles and stories.

Look again at the chart. How many of the items there can be identified as key strands in literature, in myth, legend, fable, in fantasy and reality, in poem, short story and novel? Children may not make the link between the storyline and aspects of bullying, the prevention of bullying or the dealing with threatening situations – you could make these links for them and then, later, with them.

Bullying is not really one issue, since it involves problem solving, assertiveness and a whole host of other factors and skills. A great many sensitive issues can be approached through children's literature. No one story can address the bullying problem; it needs

> *Children may not make the link between the storyline and aspects of bullying, the prevention of bullying or the dealing with threatening situations – you could make these links for them and then, later, with them*

to be tackled in the curriculum beginning with the youngest child and reworked and revisited through every age and stage. Literature is a core component of the English curriculum, making it a good vehicle for exploring with children all kinds of behaviour, including aspects of bullying and being bullied, of witnessing bullying, participating or ignoring it, as well as determining to tackle it. Good literature offers a wealth of opportunities, not only within the English and PSE curriculum (especially with the introduction of literacy hour), but also within drama and PE.

It is vital to begin by choosing good literature. This makes it difficult but it is very important. Perhaps the first thing is to clarify what we mean by literature. It is something about the quality of the language and, in many children's books, the illustrations, the way the language draws the reader into the story, makes the reader care about the characters, feel for them, with them or even against them. It is something about the fact that the characters, when they come to the end of the story, have learned something, about themselves, or other people, or the world around them.

The author must not be patronising to the reader and while offering much, must still leave space for the reader to construct his or her own pictures, sounds and feelings. The story must not cheat by bringing in a new character at the end to solve everyone's problems and preferably it must end on a positive note!

When a book is chosen, only the teacher will know what works with this class at this moment, what grips them, what makes them say, 'Read it again, read it again, don't stop'. A story must be chosen for its quality and language then. Then, and only then, is it time to look at it in terms of tackling issues around bullying and being bullied.

There is a real danger in choosing a story or book that declares itself as being a book about bullying. The listener will know within thirty seconds that it is a would-be moral, edifying tale; not a story for story-lovers but a way of 'getting at you' about bullying. They recognise such a story very quickly and in the first thirty seconds of reading it you have probably lost them, if you ever had them.

With a good story, you might like to try some of these ideas:

- Look in the story. Where does a character have to deal with a situation? Is it a situation involving the character directly or involving friends or family?
- How does the character deal with the situation? Who helps, how does the character get help, how does he or she choose the person to ask or tell? Could the character have chosen another strategy, done something different or asked someone else?
- Look at the outcome. How was it related to what the character decided to do? What other outcomes were possible?

- **Look at critical moments in the story. Try drawing the story line noting the important steps. Find all the critical moments. Look at the alternative endings and how all the characters would feel at the outcome of each ending.**
- **Choose a step, a critical moment on the way. How did the characters feel at that moment? What were they thinking, saying or not saying? If you had been there, watching, out of sight, how would you have felt? If you had been closer, what might you have said, felt, done or not done?**

Now think about other situations: if the storyline had instead presented a problem about bullying, rework the story applying the same questions.

Don't condemn picture books to the infant stage. They are often too sophisticated for very young children and their stories are often

Don't condemn picture books to the infant stage. They are often too sophisticated for very young children and their stories are often very deep

very deep. Use strategies which invite older children to think how such stories could be applied to other problems, including bullying.

Whenever you have finished a discussion of the story, chapter extract, read it through to bring back its completeness after analysing it.

Remember good stories are like onions, they can be peeled and peeled, always revealing or offering something new to find.

Drama

Drama offers a wealth of opportunities including role playing difficult situations, keeping feelings under control, resisting pressures and practising the expression of strong emotions. Teachers skilled in interactive drama have found by using one small group to develop a situation that an audience can then use it to experiment with possible alternate strategies or endings and this can be a powerful means of exploring bullying.

Children need to learn the best ways, the best times and the best people to tell if they need help. They need to feel confident with the language of telling and this needs both building up and practice. A simple activity is to allow children time to keep a personal record of their feelings, actions, reflections and progress.

PHYSICAL EDUCATION

PE can contribute to preventing bullying by helping young people gain physical confidence and greater self control. It can also offer opportunities to work together and to support one another. The contribution of PE needs to be carefully managed, because failure (particularly public failure) at sports can serve to further isolate and humiliate vulnerable young people.

Conclusion

So how have you arrived here? Perhaps, if you are right handed and you are flicking through this book, this may be the first page you have read, perhaps you have just dipped in and pulled ideas out to try in your school, or perhaps you have read the whole book from page one through to here (in which case, well done!).

However you used this book, we hope you have found it useful. Like so many topics within education, we are all learning from one another all the time, but even more important is the learning we uncover by working with children.

Unless we see the world through their eyes and try to make and then maintain a link with their feelings, it is very easy to forget the huge and diverse range of experiences each child brings to our classroom. If the goal of your school is to continually improve the quality of teaching and learning that is taking place, bullying is an issue that simply cannot be ignored. If the goal of education is to support the creation of civilised people who can live and work together constructively, we ignore bullying at our peril.

Bibliography

Elliot M 1992
'Bullies, victims, signs and solutions' in
Bullying: A Practical Guide to Coping for Schools
Ed Elliot M, Longman

Olweus D 1984
'Aggressors and their victims: bullying in schools' in
Disruptive Behaviour in Schools
Ed Frude N & Gault H, Wiley, New York

Jones E 1992
**'Practical considerations in dealing with bullying in
secondary school'** in *Bullying: A Practical Guide to
Coping for Schools*
Ed Elliot M, Longman

Fine A 1993
The Angel of Nitshill Road
Mammoth

Kolb DA 1984
*Experiential Learning: Experience as a Source of
Learning and Development*
2nd Edition Englewood Cliffs NJ, Prentice Hall

Watkins C Cornell E, Lodge C and Whalley C 1996
Effective Learning
SIN Research Mattrs, Institute Of Education, University of London

TACADE
Skills for Adolescence

Feeling Good

by Noreen Wetton and Peter Cansell

Feeling Good is a humorous guide to raising the self-esteem of even the youngest child and most beleaguered teacher – and improving the learning and teaching processes.

- Dozens of activities, strategies and exercises
- Illustrated throughout
- Helpful real-life examples
- Top-selling book to hold on to and annotate throughout your career

About the authors:

Noreen Wetton was previously director of the HEA's Primary Health Education Project, and has written and lectured widely from the Health Education Unit at Southampton University.

Peter Cansell has taught in Oxfordshire and is now a pastoral tutor and an English and Humanities teacher at Frideswide Middle School, Oxford.

ISBN 0 901762 93 8   68pp   Price £6.50

For copies of *Feeling Good*, contact Forbes Publications at Abbott House, 1-2 Hanover Street, London W1R 9WB
Tel 0171 495 7945 Fax 0171 495 7916

 **fp** FORBES PUBLICATIONS

Keeping Safe

A Programme of Safety Education for Young Children

by Margaret Collins – author of *Let's Get it Right For Nursery Children*

Safety skills cannot be learnt too early. This book, packed with practical lesson ideas, will instil safety habits to last a lifetime.

Concern for the safety of young children is constantly in the minds of parents and teachers. Safety education is increasingly important, yet often it is left until key stage 2.

This innovative book contains ideas and lesson plans for children at key stage 1. Margaret Collins' direct classroom experience shows that effective safety education can be taught to young children and this book demonstrates practical ideas and techniques for achieving this.

Safety in the home, using electricity and gas, on the railway, in the car, on water, with fire – all these and more are covered in this inspiring book. Every primary school should have a copy.

ISBN 1 899527 02 8   87pp   Price £7.95

For copies of *Keeping Safe*, contact Forbes Publications at Abbott House, 1-2 Hanover Street, London W1R 9WB

Tel 0171 495 7945 Fax 0171 495 7916

fp FORBES PUBLICATIONS

Playing Around

Activities and Exercises for Social and Cooperative Learning

by Susan Rowe and Susan Humphries
Illustrations by Carol Holliday

This book is a storehouse of games, activities and exercises for young children designed to promote social and cooperative learning by teaching children to work together. It is essential that children learn how to work together effectively and as a team: the aim of *Playing Around* is to promote team work and cooperative class work.

The authors have given many courses and lectures on their work and *Playing Around* is a result of their experiences.

ISBN 0 901762 96 2   92pp   Price £6.95

For copies of *Playing Around*, contact Forbes Publications at Abbott House, 1-2 Hanover Street, London W1R 9WB

Tel 0171 495 7945 Fax 0171 495 7916

fp F O R B E S   P U B L I C A T I O N S

After the Ark

Religious understandings of ourselves and other animals

By Martin Palmer and Elizabeth Breuilly

For teachers and students of religion and PSE, and those leading school assemblies.

- 90 activities

- Stories, poems, information boxes, multi-faith scriptural passages, discussion points

- Suitable for classroom sessions, discussions, individual and group project work, and homework

- Seven complete assembly plans and ideas for more

An inspiring exploration of humanity's relationship with animals - seen from a multi-faith and multi-cultural perspective. This is a book for use in assemblies, in pastoral care and in religious studies.

Taking the viewpoints of various religious faiths, the authors illustrate how different religions have different attitudes to animals, and how each is valuable in its own way.

ISBN 1 899527 03 6   96pp   Price £8.95

For copies of *After the Ark*, **contact Forbes Publications at Abbott House, 1-2 Hanover Street, London W1R 9WB**

Tel 0171 495 7945 Fax 0171 495 7916

 **FORBES PUBLICATIONS**

Tel: 0171 495 7945 Fax: 0171 495 7916 | Abbott House 1–2 Hanover Street London W1R 9WB | Please return to: Forbes Publications

Title	ISBN	Price	Quantity	Total per title
Schools Without Fear	1 899527 12 5	£6.95		
Let's Get It Right For Nursery Children	1 899527 13 3	£6.95		
Making Grammar Fun	1 899527 01 X	£7.50		
Feeling Good	0 901762 93 8	£6.50		
Keeping Safe	1 899527 02 8	£7.95		
Working Together	1 899527 04 4	£7.95		
Playing Around	0 901762 96 2	£6.95		
Eat Your Words	1 874279 07 1	£9.95		
Sex Education in Primary schools	1 899527 00 1	£6.95		
Teaching AIDS in the classroom	0 901762 95 4	£12.50		
Smack or Sympathy	1 899527 07 9	£ 6.95		
The Health Promoting School	1 899527 05 2	£12.95		
Health for Life	0 901762 98 9	£10.50		
Health & Self pack	0 901762 85 7	£54.95		
Health & Self Introductory Handbook	0 901762 86 5	£6.95		
Marketing Your School	1 899527 06 0	£8.95		
Towards 2000	1 899527 09 5	£12.95		
After the Ark	1 899527 03 6	£8.95		
Compassionate Farming	1 899527 14 1	£5.95		
The Big Science Books				
All About Living	0 901762 91 1	£12.95		
Materials and Forces	0 901762 92 X	£12.95		
Science Experiments in Food and Textiles	0 901762 97 0	£15.95		
The Science and Technology of Foods	0 901762 93 0	£16.50		
Technology of Textile Properties	0 901762 82 2	£16.50		

Add p&p £1.95

TOTAL £ _____

☐ I enclose a cheque made payable to
Forbes Publications for £_____
☐ Please invoice: I enclose an official order
Order No _____
☐ Please debit my:
Mastercard ☐ Visa ☐ Amex ☐ Diners Card ☐
Total £_____
Card No
|__|__|__|__|__|__|__|__|__|__|__|__|__|__|__|__|__|
Card expiry date
____ / ____ /

Name _____
Organisation _____
Address _____
_____
_____
_____
Postcode _____
Tel _____
Signature _____
Date _____

Chris d'Lacey

A Break in the Chain

Illustrated by
JOANNA CAREY

YELLOW BANANAS

For
Boley, Fizz and Sunshine